BEHIND THE EUROCENTRIC VEILS

BEHIND THE EUROCENTRIC VEILS

THE SEARCH FOR AFRICAN REALITIES

CLINTON M. JEAN

Foreword by James Jennings

The University of Massachusetts Press

AMHERST

Printed in the United States of America
LC 91-22685
ISBN 0–87023–757–8
Designed by Jack Harrison
Set in Garamond by Keystone Typesetting, Inc.
Printed and bound by Thomson-Shore, Inc.

Library of Congress Cataloging-in-Publication Data
Jean, Clinton M. (Clinton Michael).
    Behind the Eurocentric veils : the search for African realities /
Clinton M. Jean ; foreword by James Jennings.
        p.   cm.
    Includes bibliographical references.
    ISBN 0–87023–757–8
    1. Ethnology—Africa, Sub-Saharan—Philosophy.
2. Ethnocentrism—Europe.   3. Africa, Sub-Saharan—Historiography.
4. Africa, Sub-Saharan—Civilization.   I. Title.
GN645.J42   1991
305.8'0096—dc20   91–22685
                                                                CIP

British Library Cataloguing in Publication data are available.

This book is published with the support and cooperation of the University of
Massachusetts at Boston

Acknowledgment is made to the following publishers for permission to
reprint excerpts from their books:

The Free Press, a division of Macmillan, Inc., from Max Weber, *The Theory
of Social and Economic Organization,* trans. A. M. Henderson and Talcott
Parsons, ed. Talcott Parsons, © 1947, © renewed 1975 by Talcott
Parsons.
HarperCollins Publishers, from Ignazio Silone, in *The God That Failed,* ed.
Richard Crossman, © 1949 by Ignazio Silone; © 1949 by Richard
Crossman.
International Publishers, from Karl Marx, *Pre-Capitalist Economic Formations,*
ed. E. J. Hobsbawm.
Lawrence Hill Books, Brooklyn, N.Y., from Cheikh Anta Diop, *The African
Origin of Civilization: Myth or Reality,* © 1974 Lawrence Hill Books.

For Quentin Michael Jean
  Chrissandra Marie Jean
  Marla Winter
  Ishaq Eric Jean

My children—for the blessings they have brought me.
May God bless them.

CONTENTS

FOREWORD

AS AMERICA approaches the end of the millen-
nium, it finds itself at *the* critical, historical crossroads in black/
white relations. The validity of the proposition that this nation
has reached a "post–civil-rights" period of equality and good
will can be and, in fact, is being questioned. Explanations for
the continuing social, economic, and educational gaps between
blacks and whites are being debated in scholarly, political, and
civic arenas. What can no longer be questioned—and this is
what I mean when I say that America is at the critical racial
crossroads of its history—is that race relations in our society,
which have previously gone unreconciled, now must be resolved.

We have yet to achieve the "beloved community" envisioned
by Dr. Martin Luther King, Jr. He claimed that for the nation to
move forward in a state of health, it had to seek and finally
achieve racial reconciliation based on social justice. This just
resolution will not be possible, however, as long as the development of American society and the experiences of blacks both
inside and outside that society are viewed from "behind Eurocentric veils" imposed by the Western intellectual tradition.

Part of the reason Americans have not yet come to racial reconciliation is because our country's political and social institutions,

and especially its prestigious intellectual ones, have ignored or denied the potential and power of the African consciousness—whether manifest or latent—within black life in America. This means, as Clinton Jean writes, "that Third World cultures are falsely identified as moving along the same historical evolutionary path as the West, propelled by the same cultural ideals and the same dynamic forces . . . well within the Eurocentric boundaries of Western historical experiences." Consequently, what can be called the African part, or things African, of blacks in America has been continually denied.

Such systematic denial has a long tradition in the white intellectual community. This denial was encapsulated by journalist Mike Wallace in the fifties, when he presumed to explain to the black playwright Lorraine Hansberry that blacks were merely "ersatz whites." This attitude was summarized by sociologist Nathan Glazer in the sixties, when he claimed that Negroes in America had no culture that they could call their own. And this denial is evident today in the vast, indeed overwhelming, number of educational institutions that either ignore the positive, empowering, different attitudes and ideas blacks can bring to the marketplace of ideas or perversely choose to define those different things as inferior.

For America to become in principle *and* practice a pluralistic, democratic society, and for our nation to again become economically productive, it is necessary to acknowledge that a group of people numbering in the tens of millions has to be included as an equal partner in the current and future unfolding of America's society and political economy. True acceptance and appreciation will mean that blacks can move forward with a healthy balance between their African heritage and the heritage resulting from four hundred years of residence and resistance on the North American continent—the overwhelming majority of those years, of course, spent in slavery.

In this stimulating book, Clinton Jean examines and critiques the Eurocentric bias in both the liberal and Marxist intellectual traditions in Western thought. He does so from a consciously

African-centered perspective. It should be pointed out that this approach, which is here referred to as Afrocentrism, is not a new one. In fact, Jean's study is part of a rich and developing heritage in the history of black thought. The contributions of such black intellectuals, writers, and activists as W. E. B. Du Bois, Booker T. Washington, Ida B. Wells Barnett, Arturo Schomburg, Martin Luther King, Jr., Malcolm X, Ron Karenga, Sonia Sanchez, Wade Nobles, Molefi Kete Asante and the work and art of many others are part of this continuum of African-centered thought—a continuum that Clinton Jean joins with publication of this book.

Beyond its merits as an intellectual/theoretical exercise, this book has many implications for higher education and public policy. An African-centered perspective can provide a "resource for the creative restructuring of the social order." For example, this book forces us to reconsider what we mean by "excellence" in American higher education, and whether this excellence can be achieved within a framework limited by Eurocentric assumptions and biases.

Jean's book also has implications for public policy regarding the social well-being of the black community in this society. Many, and I include myself in their number, have started to suggest that in delivering human and educational services to the black community, an African-centered perspective can be effective in resolving the social and economic problems that face this community. There has been a resurgence of interest in recent years, for instance, in starting community schools for black youth in order to give them an understanding and appreciation of African-centered culture and behaviors. These efforts should be continued and expanded.

Perhaps the most important contribution of this book is the author's analytical and eloquent reminder that "African traditions . . . are not fossilized artifacts in the historical consciousness." And, furthermore, that "these traditions are the necessary foundation of black identity within the American ethnic mix." This is a proposition that blacks have had continually to embrace in order to survive in America. But today it is also imperative for *whites* to understand this idea and, by understanding the significance and validity of Afrocentricity in the life of black America, finally to overcome the artificial and arrogant intellectual confinement that has limited white American thinking and creativity.

James Jennings
William Monroe Trotter Institute
University of Massachusetts at Boston

PREFACE

THE ARGUMENT that follows is posed as a scholarly exercise. But it did not originate and evolve in the realm of pure scholarship. It was rooted in all I came to experience as a foreign black (from Trinidad) in America.

I once read somewhere that all blacks are colonized. No doubt. Still not all are colonized in the same way. The Mighty Sparrow was right: "All o' we is one"—that applies to all blacks beyond the Caribbean. The fact is, though, all of us are different too. Thrust into that difference, I came to discover what it was to be black in America.

It was quite a thing to be surrounded by white people. Now, in Trinidad, we all grew up hearing, "White alright; Brown stand around; Black fall back." And Asian Indians, the other large group of color in Trinidad, were dismissed by a legion of uncomplimentary epithets, attitudes, and racial myths. But the blackness all around probably shielded consciousness from the mortal lesions of those poisons. Black midwives, black godparents, black barbers, black market people, black union people, black professionals, black teachers, black nationalist leaders, black soccer players, black musicians—all these were living proof of a fluid and adaptive social intelligence in the race that could solve any human riddle. Nor were Indians a backward crowd of rural idiots. They fed the country, produced entrepreneurs in local business, filled the growing ranks of the professionals, gave stalwart leadership in the struggles of working people, articulated creative agendas on national political issues, gave birth to and nurtured a world-renowned novelist (Vidia Naipaul). More important, the communal traditions that had governed Africans and Indians throughout their history were as vibrant as they had always been. Against numerically preponderant populations of blacks and Indians locked into their ancestral cultures, white power, emanating from the distance of the British colonial office, could not impose or attempt total control over its Trinidadian subjects. In America, however, as I came to find out, white power had taken a different course. It wasn't a joke when they said "this is white man's country."

My first encounters with white people gave no promise of anything unpleasant to come. I bore no suspicions toward them. Indeed there was an excited energy in meeting new people and adventuring with them into the surge of the political and social upheavals of the sixties. I enjoyed the personal interchanges, the mutual discovery of shared interests. Thank God, I made lasting attachments and friendships. The times, they were a'changing. How could I know that? I thought what I saw was all simply part of the normal plan. In the more formal settings of institutional life, though, I came to sense an undertow of different traditional practices, those that had made America white.

Columbia University, to a newcomer, seemed hardly a place that would offer haven to ethnocentric bias, and racism as one expression of that. I had occasional exposure to bigotry outside the school while job hunting and searching for apartments. Those encounters were crass and, since they were face-to-face, obvious. Things were not that obvious at the university, even where encounters were face-to-face. The university was, after all, a refuge and a symbol of enlightenment and learning.

In time, under the political assaults of the struggle for civil rights and the antiwar movement, the image of the ivory tower collapsed—abruptly at Columbia, with student occupation of campus buildings. The publication of documents liberated from the files of several administrations revealed the interlock between the major universities and the dominant institutions—corporations, government, the military. An outcry was raised against a proposal by Columbia to build a gymnasium in Morningside Park—it was regarded by student radicals as an unwanted occupation of the Harlem community that would bring no benefit to Harlem residents. The demand for open enrollment in higher education, one product of the civil rights struggle, touched an especially vulnerable nerve at the university. There were very few black American students at the school, and even fewer black faculty and administrators. I knew of one black professor in anthropology; most black people that I met were either from Africa or the Caribbean.

All these confrontations were reflected in intellectual debates exercising opposing schools of social thought. In sociology, my field of study, unrest set functionalists, who claimed Weber as their most important mentor, against avowed Marxists. Debate focused on a particular question. Was it values that held social systems together and directed them on their course through history? Or, was it antagonistic material interests that drove historical motion? In the logic of that reality, wasn't power, and its instrumentalities, the real linchpin of the social order?

There were related questions on a more empirical level, questions addressed to specific matters of historical fact. Was capitalism a product of a set of values peculiar to the West? Or, was it produced by material forces—enclosures, dispossession of the landed poor, appropriation of church lands, colonialism?

The Marxists chose power. It seemed to me they had a point, especially with regard to the colonial situation. It could hardly be said that colonies were tied to the "mother country" by value consensus. Consistent with that, one could make an argument that formal national independence had made them into neocolonies. They weren't underdeveloped simply because they lacked the requisite values that could propel them into industrial takeoff.

Liberal thought—whether as functionalism, theories of pluralist democracy, bourgeois theories of underdevelopment (and development)—did not stand in the arena of contending discourse as just another participant. It did not depend only on the force of evidence. It was and is the ideological arm of corporate liberal power. It did not give ground. The primacy of values remained an axiom.

But really, I thought, didn't liberals have a point? Didn't values play a prime role in all human action? It could be demonstrated beyond question that being determines consciousness, as the Marxists would say. Still it was impossible to imagine any human group acting without ideas. Values determined what use would be made of being, all existent things, human forces, and all natural forces. If the problem was framed as a choice between material forces and values (ideas) as the prime motor of history, then the problem was insoluble.

One could read history differently. Material stresses in feudal economy had certainly created or enlarged the bourgeois classes and brought them and their ideas to power. But then the bourgeois made the world according to their vision of it. Ideas may not make history out of whole cloth. If people think of it, though, they may make the cloth.

Figuring all this out was one of my earliest moments of sociological clarity in graduate school. It took time identifying the contending schools of thought in terms of their basic assumptions. My own assumptions weren't clear either. But I knew what attracted me. I was more interested in history, or a sense of history (as with Durkheim, Weber, Marx), than in rules of scientific method and scientific systems of analysis. There was something uncomfortable—suspect, even invalid, I would say later—about exactness, at least as liberal social science defined it. By the liberal formula my interest in oriental humanities, Western philosophy, Perez Galdós was acceptable only as exposure to the arts and humanities. It was not acceptable I was told explicitly, more often implicitly, if I was looking to these disciplines for scientifically valid pictures of human behavior. I didn't have a ready counterargument to this. But I found myself seeking the unification of intellectual worlds regarded as incompatible at Columbia.

I felt the assumed opposition between the hard and soft sides of social thought was a mistake—as was the opposition the liberals posed between values and material forces. Did anyone doubt the fidelity to social reality of the world reproduced in Arthur Koestler's *Darkness at Noon?* Who would deny that the experience of Richard Wright (and others unknown) with the American Communist party finds accurate reflection in Ralph Ellison's *Invisible Man?* One could do so only if one wanted to deny that the distrust with which the Party leadership greeted Wright's interest in the lives and vision of black workers is exactly reflected in Brother Jack's arrogant reprimand of the black protagonist for pursuing similar interests. No, the world of thinking wasn't that divisible after all. Precision could and did emanate from the soft side of social thought.

It was turning out that some questions I had about liberal social science weren't quite the same as those the Marxists had. I had to find answers that could not come from the Marxist camp. There were questions I never posed verbally—or even posed at all in a consciously explicit way. I was interested in the fate of colonies and found Marxism a very useful tool in probing colonial history. But I wasn't a Marxist. I didn't identify myself as such, as Marxists tended primarily to do. My interest in Marxism simply had a certain accord with my circumstances. I was a colonial—and bourgeois sociology did not properly address my concerns. I accepted arts and humanities as windows on the human scene as much as science was. But then I had never distinguished myth and fiction from reality. Of course, I knew that Xenophon was "real" and Heracles, Medea, and the Deerslayer were not—I met them in high school. Still, they all spoke equally of places where life was full and living was adventure. Liberal sociology never got close to that fullness by its own choice and self-definition. In my exploration of sociology these conceptions were expressed less as questions than as life-style.

Life-style was a visible, abiding aspect of political-ideological posture. It was ground for camaraderie; it was ground for distance. In public everybody acknowledged that. It was not acknowledged at the university, where tradition required that dialogue accord strictly with rules of proof and disproof. It would have been better if the significance of life-style had been acknowledged. Even without open acknowledgment though, as ideological commitments hardened, it could be seen that behind their passionless tones—accepted sign of objective, value-free analysis—liberal intellectuals concealed the emotional, political, and moral fervors that characterize engagé proselytizers. Departmental distemper was not manifested in outrage. It was expressed as decisions. (As a senior faculty member once said to me, "You might think we're all shits here; but we have the power.")

The department cleaned house. There was a similar housecleaning in the wider political arena as the spring of '68, the moment of student revolts, disappeared into the political mists. Many white friends, all of the radical set, departed the scene. I was required to write a terminal master's thesis. If it were good enough, I was told, I would be admitted to doctoral candidacy.

A Guyanese friend, a woman with strong nationalist sentiments, whispered something in my ear: my social life didn't sit well with the folks that counted, all white men dealing with a black man who didn't seem to know his place. I wasn't convinced. I was determined that the thesis would make my case.

The response was negative. But I was never able to get an adequate critique of the thesis—which dealt with the rhythms of colonization and decolonization in my native Trinidad. I will not dwell on details, but I became convinced that, despite my *magna cum laude* status as a graduate of the School of General Studies at Columbia, my work was not receiving a fair review as an intellectual product. Ultimately I won candidacy in the doctoral program with the help of two scholars in my department.

This whole experience—there were others that followed at Columbia and, later, at Brandeis where I completed my degree under more tolerable circumstances—cut my ties to the mainstream. I lost innocence in the conflict of interpretation, of style and of purpose, and in the frictions of personal encounters. I was left with a bleakly dishonorable picture of liberal scholarship, which, despite its pretensions, seemed neither objective nor free of downright bias.

Bias, I understood very well, was not just something that was directed against me personally. It sprung from an assumption that liberal formulas—*Eurocentric* formulas, period—were the universal benchmark by which to judge the worth of all cultural practices. It was always surprising when white friends, even those from the hip left, said they thought the Stones were more danceable than James Brown, or that Miles Davis derived from Chet Baker. They had no feeling for Celia Cruz and Sonora Matancera, Tito Puente, and Willie Bobo. Very few seemed to know who Charlie Parker was. How could they call Paul Whiteman the king of jazz when Louis Armstrong was on the scene? And if they thought Dave Brubeck's "Take Five" was so original, why didn't they feel the same way about Max Roach and Sonny Rollins's "Valse Hot"? Without the slightest apparent twitch of conscience Europeans had destroyed entire peoples—there was not a single Tasmanian left alive on the planet. All this in the name of Western progress—materialistic frenzy; the use of human energy, knowledge, and science in a progressive and unyielding dismemberment of human beings and the natural order; a toxic narcissism; and the divorce of action from humane morality.

The entire corpus of mainstream social thought (including even Marxism and modern feminism, with their own peculiar disagreement with the mainstream) preaches this kind of progress as a universal, axiomatic absolute. In the American education system all cultures, we are told, espouse it. The system, by the simple device of instilling a warped vision, or no vision at all, of their cultural history in the consciousness of black peoples has, I have come to believe, produced generations of puppets, lap dogs, house niggers, "slaves who take gifts from their masters" (remember Denmark Vesey?), and black bourgeois mentalities seeking fulfillment in the ownership of Olds Cutlass Cieras.

Some colonials, though, have been possessed by an aboriginal cultural memory with the life persistence of the phoenix. Marvin Harris in *Cows, Pigs, Wars, and Witches* has told us of native Australians who, through the maze of Western deceit, recognized the unholy greed of their conquerors. Here in America the works of E. Franklin Frazier, W. E. B. DuBois, and Toni Morrison are a reservoir of knowledge that tells who we really are. And for Africans everywhere, there has appeared an intellect that offers the most complete promise of the richest intellectual possibilities for our time, in the late Cheikh Anta Diop. Among the heirs to the vision of the resurrected African past he has bequeathed to us in works such as *The African Origin of Civilization,* we must count Ivan Van Sertima (*They Came Before Columbus*) and Molefi K. Asante (*The Afrocentric Idea*). This book is also a contribution to that Afrocentric effort.

Acknowledgments

I am indebted to the members of my Brandeis University dissertation committee, Professor Maurice Stein, Professor Egon Bittner, and Professor Irving Zola, and to the outside reader, Professor James Jennings, for their constructively critical intellectual support. I am especially indebted to the chair, Professor Stein, for his sympathetic understanding; and to Professor Jennings for keeping me aware that my research was appearing in a context of black scholarship that is searching and original. I thank Eileen Julien for her careful and attentive reading of the manuscript and for her provocative suggestions. I wish to thank Paul Wright, University of Massachusetts Press editor, for his unflagging encouragement and editorial assistance; Pam Wilkinson and Catlin Murphy of the Press staff, for guiding the book through the production process; and Brenda Hanning, who painstakingly copyedited the text.

I owe immeasurable gratitude to Deborah Agostini, Brenda Wolcott, Anneke Corbett, Steve Terry, June Gordon, and Gerry Scott—all friends who sustained me through difficult travails. I am deeply thankful to my wife, Denise Dabney Jean, who graciously typed and edited the dissertation manuscript upon which this book is based.

BEHIND
THE
EUROCENTRIC
VEILS

INTRODUCTION

ELEANOR BURKE Leacock notes that anthropology has misrepresented the position of women in primitive human society (the band) by assuming that male dominance exists in this early period.[1] Her ethnographic descriptions, gleaned from missionary accounts of the lifeways of Montagnais-Naskapi Indians before European penetration, indicate that this is a false conclusion. Such a conclusion can stand only if one ignores the impact of the European presence on Algonkian culture: European intrusion transformed the sexually egalitarian relations of native Amerindian cultures. Thus, sociocultural evolution as it actually happened is misinterpreted by theories that misrepresent the position of women in primitive society and ignore the decisive effect of European incursion on primitive sexual equality. It follows that there is a need to rethink mainstream anthropological theory where it addresses these questions.

She also observes that Marxist analysis, the other important tradition in contemporary social thought, similarly suffers from theoretical and practical (political) weakness when it addresses a parallel problem: racial and national oppression within the modern European hegemony. Distortion occurs where the development of modern capitalism is treated as a phenomenon separate "from racist brutality and national oppression throughout its history." By ignoring this interconnectedness the Marxian tradition lost sight of what Marx himself revealed: that "the nature of exploitation itself as a principle . . . was and is colorless, raceless, and sexless." Ultimately theoretical myopia crystallized in the definition of exploitation "as centrally of whites and of men."[2] And, in America at least, political praxis fumbled the integration of blacks as a viable and integrated force in a revolutionary socialist movement after the Second World War by dogmatically insisting that their exploitation as workers had a higher salience than their oppression as blacks.

Sociology too, like anthropology, suffers from the same weaknesses suggested in Leacock's remarks, and for the same reasons, in its interpretation of Third World cultures in general and African cultures in particular. The chapters that follow will define the theoretical inadequacy of liberal sociology in these areas. They will also argue, as Leacock does, that the Marxist tradition has indeed misconstrued Third World history. As we will see, misinterpretation begins with Marx and Engels themselves.

The principal thesis advanced in this book is that Third World cultures are falsely identified as moving along the same historical evolutionary path as the West, propelled by the same cultural ideals and the same dynamic forces. Both the liberal and Marxist systems subsume Third World cultural processes under universalist theories of evolution that do not apply universally. Each system, of course, has its distinctive comparative-historical model—they assess the destructive impact of Western culture on the Third World differently—but both stay well within the ethnocentric boundaries of Western historical experience.

Chapter one offers a critical exposition of the liberal theory of cultural evolution as it applies to the Third World before and since European contact. This theory depends on a paradigm rooted in Hegel and Weber; articulated for modern sociology, with seminal revision, by Parsons; and designed for concrete application in underdeveloped societies and "culturally deprived minority" communities by liberal theorists of Third World development.

To what extent does the Marxian tradition offer a more accurate interpretation of Third World cultural identity and evolution? This is the question discussed in the second chapter. Whatever the merits of the Marxian criticism of the liberal notion that capitalism is the permanent end of history, Marxism does not understand Third World cultures as heterogeneously different from the West. Theoretical misunderstanding translated into the creation and application of programs to transform the Third World—as part of the world that Marxism wanted not just to understand but to change—which Third World peoples criticized as inappropriate to their circumstances or abandoned in organizational practice. Some reference will be made to the fate of these programs among African peoples in Africa and elsewhere in the world, especially in America.

In the discussion that follows, interest is expressed in the Third World as a whole, but Africa and African peoples receive special emphasis. If neither liberalism nor Marxism comprehends Africa, clearly an *Afro*centric view of history—at least of African culture and history—is required. The burden of the third chapter is to present such a view. It will attempt to show that African traditions have different motivations and consequences from Western traditions. This chapter represents an emphatic assertion of the existence of a multicultural universe on the planet. It suggests moreover that history, seen from a multicultural perspective, might well reveal models of living that could solve many of our modern social dilemmas. And it contributes to the ongoing restoration of African cultural-historical identity, which has been under assault for some time.

What leads to critical rethinking of intellectual traditions? What led to the critical rethinking proposed here? Eleanor Leacock states that in addition to a scientific basis she had what she calls a "personal/political basis" for her disagreement with the thesis of universal male dominance. Hers, she says, was an angry disagreement: her personal life, embracing motherhood and professional (as an anthropologist) as well as radical political activity, daily contradicted theories of female passivity; and she was well aware that being a woman had everything to do with her not being able to earn a decent income. She was also aware, however, that as much as personal experience may have informed her understanding, disproving the thesis of universal male dominance required scientific research into the position of women in history. Personal experience alone would not prove her case; and scientific tradition would certainly consider such evidence inelegant.

Her discovery of disconfirming historical/cultural evidence was, she says, unexpected considering that she had heard, and accepted, the thesis of male preeminence from a thinker she respected as a student. But it could hardly have been purely intellectual accident. It is surely reasonable to assume that personal experience created the sensitivity that enabled her to recognize data, however unexpectedly discovered, as evidence of disconfirmation. Others, themselves authorities but with a different personal experience, had missed those very data, and not because they had not encountered them.

As I suggested, personal experience, in scientific judgment, is considered an inelegant datum and basis for scientific conclusions. But, it is necessary to insist, such experience has no inherent negative bearing on the scientific character and validity of social analysis even if it is acknowledged as the impulse that generates research. Any negative bearing on scientific objectivity is assumed. Supposedly, personal experience is the door through which values and value judgments enter science, a thing that is anathema to moderns.

The sociology of knowledge can actually reveal the historical origins of the principle that Western science has to be value-free. It can reveal that the principle, far from being ordained as eternal truth, is very much part of forces created in the political arena—that is to say, it inhabits the ideological terrain. Invented as a device to free science from political convenience the value-free principle has evolved to a different purpose: it has come to legitimize the separation of morality from science. On this basis, scientific inquiry can now claim and defend its right to espouse any end.

But the results of social-scientific inquiry fall squarely in the realm of morality: inherently the social consequences of inquiry raise moral questions. By disclaiming the need and, by extension, the responsibility and even the authority to appraise morally what it does, inquiry is always only partially completed. Morality has an uncomfortable way of insisting on its place. It enters the halls of inquiry, not as honored comember, but as personal experience and the consequent ethical-political conviction—unwelcome guest in the house of science.

What has been said suggests that personal experience is one pathway to scientific inquiry and understanding, and there are other reasons to take it seriously. Merely as exposition such intellectual biography reveals how puzzles were encountered and why reigning models of explanation seemed unable to solve them. Additionally, it offers ground for the development of a significant insight: that personal problems, to recall a thoughtful intellect, are social issues.

Personal experience also contributes to what one might call an unofficial ethnology of the personal itineraries of Third World individuals, women, and others in the limbo zone of modern life, as they wend their way through the domains of the modern academy while leading their Third World lives and particular day-to-day existences. Ethnographies of this sort would be useful for those who wish to begin to see such itineraries from the inside. And for science, lost, as I have argued, in an amoral landscape, they may show the way to reunification of the rational-ethical mind: they are a record of some of the data needed to create a moral system adequate to our time, if it is accepted that such a system must be multiculturally all-embracing.

As with Eleanor Leacock's work, the critical exercise in the chapters that follow similarly has a personal-political basis, which is suggested in the preface. The book can be read with those remarks in mind.[3]

1

MAINSTREAM THINKING AND MODERN LIFE—LIVING IN THE PRESENT AND MISINTERPRETING THE PAST

"TRADITIONAL ANGLO-SAXON intolerance is a cultural trait like any other." So said no less a figure than Ruth Benedict. [1] There can hardly be any dispute about the reality of white intolerance. It suffices to recall the dismal experiences of Third World peoples wherever they have been ensnared in the white embrace. The conquistadores in the New World, the French in Haiti, the British in India, the Dutch in Indonesia, the Boers in South Africa, and the Anglo-Saxons in North America have left grisly testament of their presence. [2] Objections cannot for good reason arise at the level of historical fact; they must begin at another level.

Is Ruth Benedict's suggestion correct that chauvinism, in its aggressive forms especially, is a derivative of Western culture? Is it peculiar to the West? If it is not so societally limited in its manifestations, is it simply a result of learning, that is to say, culture?

No satisfactory answer can be given to these questions without reference to human experience cross-culturally and historically. Comparative data are not simply the necessary evidence for confirmation or disconfirmation of theories. They nourish the historical imagination. They show that cultural formations have actually existed that have answered our most troubling contemporary realities. But is historical imagination alive within the confines of the Western hegemony?

Contending interpretations on the questions raised above fall within an arena delimited by a Western frame of reference. With few exceptions, it is Westerners, after all, who have written the histories and ethnographies of the world's peoples that stand as the official texts of the modern education system. On occasion, Western thinkers have written with accurate perception about the realities of other peoples from the inside, as it were. However, as a rule, they have not done so—nor, frankly, have they been sufficient to the task.

It is not a simple matter of malice generated by the scandalous racism of a de Gobineau or an Ulrich Bonnell Phillips or a Franklin H. Giddings. Misinterpretation equally afflicts the well intentioned ("But *I* am not racist or ethnocentric!") who speak the language of "value-neutral," "objective" science—before Parsons or since his time. Is not intention, as much as any other attitude, the plaything of social forces, power, and the advantage of position? Consider William Ryan's insight:

> The highly-charged psychological problem confronting this hypothetical progressive, charitable person [the well-intentioned, "value-neutral" observer] I am talking about is that of reconciling his own self-interest with the promptings of his humanitarian impulses. . . . The typical Victim Blamer is a middle-class person who is doing reasonably well in a material way. . . . Basically, he likes the social system pretty much the way it is, at least in broad outline . . . despite his awareness that there are abuses of that system, negative side effects, and substantial residual inequalities.[3]

But if victim blaming neatly resolves the dilemma on the mental level, it does not eliminate the social contradictions. Victim and blamer retain their social locations however much this may be (conveniently) hidden from the purview of the ideology. This, and Ryan refers us to C. Wright Mills's reminder, is the ideology of white middle-class American thought and white liberal social science. Is it any less the ideology of those American dreamers who ordinarily live within racism's institutional buffer zone?

Of course, such an ideology does not hide everything. The social structure, for one thing, is not so much obscured as it is taken for granted. This is construed as an efficacious defense of the social system that succeeds even without benefit of argument—as Ryan describes the construct in the mind of the concerned middle-class citizen.[4] This is why one does not need malice to have poor vision—though there is malice enough.

There is, however, an argument. It emerges not only in connection with the strategy of social reform espoused by victim-blamers, but also in connection with the liberal program of reconstruction for Third World life as a whole, which program has its prime origins in the condition of white power in America and Western dominance worldwide. That argument tells how Westerners defend their culture. That is its purpose. More to the point here, it also instructs as to the intellectual sources of the cross-cultural blindness of Western thinkers—a blindness that finds its way into the debate on chauvinism and human aggression. This debate, like victim blaming and theories of development, is itself anchored in the historical reality of Western supremacy.

As an offshoot of this power reality, what do theories of capitalist development tell us that is germane to the issue of the poor vision, and intolerance, of Westerners? Let me begin with nomenclature, because there is much in a name. Capitalist development referred most immediately to industrial transformation of economies. Conceived more broadly as involving other institutions—cultural values, family, class systems, polity—the process was defined as modernization. These terms did not have culturally and historically neutral referents, a point that was highlighted by another term of preferred use for some time: *Westernization*. It was an apt term denoting, as it did, the Western origins of modern life and according accurately with the historical sequence of the worldwide spread of industrialization— in the First World (the West), then in the Second World (Soviet

Russia and Eastern Europe), and more lately in the Third World (the semicolonies, colonies, and "independent" neocolonies).

Apart from sequence, chronology, where it had reference to the Third World, also suggested hierarchy. But it suggested hierarchy without reference to power. Such terms as *evolving nations, traditional cultures,* and *underdeveloped societies* referred solely to the place of the world they described in the journey toward progress. Such distortion of analytic vision produced those mistaken strategies of development in vogue today. (The central dogma in the liberal strategy calls for closer ties with metropolitan centers on the part of the Third World economies. This proposal makes little sense since such ties emerged long ago in a colonial situation, thus engendering in the process the very underdevelopment the policies are now supposed to remedy.) And it generated, as with the terms just used, a mislabeling of the phenomena of Third World life.

"Our ignorance of the underdeveloped countries' history leads us to assume that their present resembles earlier stages of the history of the now-developed countries. . . . [But] the now-developed countries were never *under*developed, though they may have been *un*developed."[5] By this criticism, André Gunder Frank meant to discourage the current style of liberal theorizing on development. He was also advising a broader revision in historical thinking.

Undeveloped—applied to the Third World the word carried a novel imagery: nonindustrial, admittedly, but certainly not preindustrial. Appropriately, it connoted a world of cultures journeying through autonomous histories that bear no relationship to the Western telos. The idea was novel, but only in the context where underdeveloped had come to designate the aboriginal state and universal starting point of cultural development—and its implicitly highest expression, modernization. The idea had been sounded before.

Ruth Benedict drew the variegated picture that is human culture in her ethnographic portraits of Zuni, Dobu, and Kwakiutl societies, impressing us with the distinctive temper of each culture. She wished to show that cultural configurations utilize only a small part of what she calls "the great arc of potential human purposes and motivations." For her, Western culture stood on the great arc along with all the other cultures, each of which stood there equal with the others. If Westerners, Americans particularly, were unaware of this variety or ignored it as a matter of habit, it was because the world of cultures had been delivered unto them. She calls our attention to the consequences:

> This world-wide [Western] cultural diffusion has protected us as man had never been protected before from having to take seriously the civilizations [cultures] of other peoples; it has given to our culture a massive universality that we have long ceased to account for historically, and which we read off rather as necessary and inevitable. We interpret our dependence, in our civilization, upon economic competition as proof that this is the prime motivation that human nature can rely upon, or we read off the behavior of small children as it is moulded in our civilization and recorded in child clinics, as child psychology or the way in which the young human animal is bound to behave. It is the same whether it is a question of our ethics or of our family organization. It is the inevitability of each familiar motivation that we defend, attempting always to identify our own local ways of behaving with Behavior, or our own socialized habits with Human Nature.

As for the costs of this ethnocentrism, she adds: "We are handicapped in dealing with human society so long as we identify our social normalities with the inevitable necessities of existence."[6]

In asserting the incommensurability—and equality—of peoples on cultural grounds Benedict was arguing that human differences can be understood as the product of conditioning. In anthropology it was a new way of looking at things, replacing an earlier paradigm that explained social phenomena on grounds of biology and race. This shift in perspective is attributed to the work of Franz Boas.

George Stocking, Jr., credits Boas with disproving some basic tenets of racial formalism in nineteenth-century anthropology: the belief in the infertility of hybrids and the stability of head form, essential elements in the dogma of the hierarchy of races. As Boas demonstrated, half-breeds (Indian-white mixtures) were more fertile than pure breeds; and head form among Jewish, Bohemian, Neapolitan, Sicilian, Polish, Hungarian, and Scottish immigrants changed intergenerationally. The most significant among his early research discoveries is the insight that the perception of vocal sounds is totally determined by culture (custom, as he was phrasing it back then). What the anthropologist in the field was accustomed to interpret in the speech of informants as lingering traces of the primitive human's first attempt to speak indicated rather the researcher's own inability to hear other peoples' vocal patterns accurately. Reared in a particular (European) language, the researcher could not apperceive all the novel sounds of strange languages. Decidedly, these sounds were not residues of the primitive utterances of our species.[7]

If culture (environment, custom) conditioned physical traits, no less did it condition mental functioning. Among human groups, thought as much as behavior was a product of tradition. The genius of a people—its ways, and particularly for Boas, its folklore—was thus historical, created, a local manifestation under circumstances of habitat and time of a "genius" evolved in the species as a whole. It was not a product of race. There was no basis for the presumption of Western superiority: "Historical events appear to have been much more potent in leading races to civilization than their faculty, and it follows that achievements of races do not warrant us to assume that one race is more highly gifted than the other." If this presumption was widely held it was because, in Stocking's paraphrase of Boas, "European civilization had cut short the promising beginnings of civilization in other areas"[8]—a thought echoing later, as we have seen, in Ruth Benedict's work.

With Boas's revolution in the science of anthropology, which penetrated the social sciences as a whole, scientific authority now stood behind the theses of the equality of races, the cultural origins of behavioral differences, and cultural relativism—a fact grasped widely, Stocking tells us, even within the general public. But if race as the determinative underpinning of behavior gave ground before the culture concept, white ethnocentric bias did not so easily yield to the perspective of relativism.[9]

It was true that old-style unilinear evolutionary theory (savagery, barbarism, civilization), the main intellectual bulwark of white ethnocentrism, could not embrace the fact of a demonstrable plurality of historically conditioned cultures. It could not claim, in particular, the unilineal evolution of family forms and psychic phenomena—art, myth, religion, philosophy, ethics. Undoubtedly, in the spheres of economy and technology human history overall showed clear sequence in its growing complexity, with the apparently independent appearance of this sequence in different cultures. But it was unwarranted to assume that these processes had been driven by the developmental unfolding of a single order of human psyche, considered savage and barbaric in its infancy and reaching its full fruition in the West.

As for World Reason—in the Hegelian formula Universal Absolute and Final Cause in the motions of history—this was nothing more than Western Reason. Hegelian metaphysics should have dissolved like some mirage created by the Western intellectual fancy, designed to obscure the many human histories not reducible to a Western measure. Yet how do we explain empirically, if not metaphysically, that the multiplicity of human histories seemed fated instead for eventual dissolution within the "massive universality" of the West? Power, of course, was the secret ingredient in this alchemy. But, like the philosopher's stone, it eluded the Western temper. Hegel himself described the aboriginal Americans as vanishing at the mere breath of the European presence. His stripes on African culture were even harsher: cannibals, traffickers in the sales of their children, primitives (heathens too) needing the civilized schooling of Western slavery. "At this point," that great philosopher—and, let us not forget, historian—says, "we leave Africa, not to mention it again." And indeed why not? "For it is no historical part of the

World; it has no movement or development to exhibit. Historical movements in it—that is in its northern part—belong to the Asiatic or European world."[10]

In the twentieth century African history (and prehistory) has been discovered; and human history is no longer defined as the manifestations of the Hegelian Absolute becoming progressively more Real. But, appropriately revised, the core of the Hegelian legacy survived the assaults of cultural relativism in the axiomatic acceptance of the West (now the modern West) as the revealed terminus of all histories; in the primacy allotted to Western history and, as a corollary, in the negation or undervaluation of other histories; in the interpretation of Western excesses, where so recognized (earlier slavery, later Modern colonialism and the African partition, still later neo-imperialism) as objective necessities of modern progress and not as an excess of power inflicted on those unwillingly subjugated; and, let us say, in a savage twist to the intellect to accommodate this reasoning. These elements constitute the working assumptions of contemporary theories of development, though they were not inherited directly from Hegel. They were filtered through the Weberian typology of authority systems and systems of administration and the schematics (the pattern variables) of Parsonian Grand Theory.

Weber affirmed the eventual universality of the Western destiny, but not because Western culture represented the climactic unfolding of the Absolute (Reason). Positivist in temper, he presented this conclusion as an inescapable induction from historical analysis, a model of thought for the empiricist style of contemporary sociology. Equally paradigmatic—and intellectually and morally exemplary—were his exclusion of racial determinism from the complex of forces that moves history, and his explicit disavowal of any suggestion of Western cultural superiority that could be drawn from the role of the West in the creation of the modern world: "The question of the relative value of the cultures which are compared here will not receive a single word."

What distinguishes Western culture, Weber observed, is its

rationalism, an organizing principle of all aspects of Western life and a trait that makes it unique among world cultures. No other culture invented a rational harmonious music based on the prescribed intervals of the major scales and amenable to reproduction because of a rational system of musical notation. Only the West produced a science based, not simply on observation, but on experiment. As in art and science, so in economy and administration—the twin foci of Weber's investigations.

It was the West that, by the development of an instrument for rational calculation (bookkeeping), transformed profit making, heretofore an activity of adventurers, into a rational economic pursuit; and reduced labor, formerly free and separated from the means of production, to a quantifiable factor of production (wages). In modern rational-legal bureaucracy Western rationalism created a system of administration technically superior to all others; and one, furthermore, that could be used in many different contexts: churches, educational institutions, private and public corporations, armies, and states. Even beyond being technically efficient and flexible as to context of application, modern bureaucracy answered the needs of mass administration in economy, government, scientific research, and voluntary associational life. It was, in fact, the necessary skeletal underpinning of modern industrial society.

The rise of industrial society outside the West signaled that rationalism was no longer a property only of Western culture. It is no surprise however that Weber, given his understanding of the place of bureaucracy within the logic of the industrial order, saw in modern bureaucratic rationalism, more than in any other aspect of industrial society (including modern capitalism), the promised fate of the world.

And what about socialist industrialism? For Weber:

> The development of the modern form of the organisation of corporate groups in all fields is nothing less than identical with the development and continual spread of bureaucratic administration. . . . Its development is, to take the most striking case, the most crucial phenomenon of the modern Western state. However

many forms there may be which do not appear to fit this pattern . . . it would be sheer illusion to think for a moment that continuous administrative work can be carried out in any field except by means of officials working in offices. . . . For bureaucratic administration is, other things being equal, always, from a formal, technical point of view, the most rational type. For the needs of mass administration today, it is completely indispensable. . . .

The primary source of the superiority of bureaucratic administration lies in the role of technical knowledge which, through the development of modern technology and business methods in the production of goods, has become completely indispensable. In this respect, it makes no difference whether the economic system is organized on a capitalistic or a socialistic basis. Indeed, if in the latter case a comparable level of technical efficiency were to be achieved, it would mean a tremendous increase in importance of specialized bureaucracy. . . .

[Additionally, to provide the communication services essential for bureaucratic efficiency] socialism would, in fact require a still higher degree of formal bureaucratization than capitalism.[11]

Bureaucratic rationalism was an inevitable end that would come when it would come. The same story, Weber would have insisted had he lived, would be told of the modernizing Third World.

All future roads would lead to the West. But Weber, unlike theorists of modernization inspired by his work, did not conceive of past histories as variations on a proto-bureaucratic phase of modern administration—although he did describe the development of bureaucracy in the West as the progressive separation of officials from the means of administration, a particular instance within Western history of the rational becoming real. The category, traditional authority, was strictly a term of comparison: traditional authority was a form different from the modern bureaucratic type, as traditional cultures on the whole differed from Western culture. These terms were preserved in cultural and economic development thinking. But while they still retained their comparative sense, they suffered an alteration of meaning: they became evolutionary stages. Traditional cultures now stood as the introductory stages to Western history.

The paradigmatic revision of Weberian terminology is the pattern variables of Talcott Parsons. Ascription-achievement, diffuseness-specificity, affectivity-neutrality, particularism-universalism, collectivity orientation-self-orientation: these elaborate the terms *traditional-rational-legal*. It is significant that they no longer apply only to interpretation of administrative systems. They now serve more broadly to characterize other subsystems and cultural formations as wholes. For instance, nonliterate societies, as Parsons calls them, do not show instrumental, political, and religiocultural complexes structurally differentiated from kin networks. In such systems social action in all institutional life follows ascriptive, diffuse, affective, particularistic patterns with the welfare of the group (collectivity) as primary. This is not so in American society where the instrumental complex is structurally differentiated from the kinship system and is indeed the structurally dominant institution. Because of its structural dominance, the patterns of social action peculiar to it penetrate and pervade all other institutions. Throughout the American system therefore social action is governed by norms of achievement, specificity, neutrality, universalism, and self-interest. America is quintessentially rational (formally). Let us remember, it is also wealthy.

American society and others like it differ from kin-based systems in degree of structural differentiation. Parsons sees beneath the structural complexity of the American social order the ascriptive beginnings of differentiation: kinship, race, ethnicity, and community still ascribe to people roles, statuses, and identities. Differentiation, though, is not only a process of complexity. More important, with Parsons, it shows direction.

Appropriately, it is in the realm of ideas that Parsons perceives direction in history. His concern is with the rise of rationalism (science) in cognitive thinking. "There seems to be no doubt," he writes, "that there is an inherent factor of the directionality of change in social systems, a directionality which was classically formulated by Max Weber in what he called the 'process of rationalization.' [There are systemic constraints that affect the spread of science.] . . . Making allowance for this factor, however, we may speak of the process of rationalization with considerable confidence as a general directional factor in the change of social systems."[12] Hence, while structural differentiation registers "the process of rationalization," rationalism in ideas determines what it will become.

The breakthrough to a rational social order is not automatic since, as mentioned, systemic forces condition the emergence of rationalization. The key is whether the instrumental complex differentiates outside kin systems or within them. Only in the former case can differentiation fully develop in the rationalist direction characteristic of advanced types of society. In the latter case, structural variation may become quite elaborate without breaking free of ascriptive-particularistic-diffuse role patterns. Parsons would attribute the failure to break free to structural obstacles, among them traditionalism.

In this conception nonliterate cultures are bound into a rationalist design in history; but within them rationalism is still-born, so to speak. Parsons cites Weber's authority for this thesis. But Weber cannot be a witness here. Let us recall that he was impressed not with how much the West resembled other cultures but with how much it differed from them. It differed precisely in its rationalism, as he was at pains to emphasize. Even if this were the result of a special kind of structural differentiation occurring in the West, it does not follow that differentiation within kin-based societies is a historical deviation. Without intellectual sleight of hand Weber's authority permits nothing more than this to be said: comparison reveals that non-Western cultures and the West are different, heterogeneous historical formations. Would it be easier to concede, if this were admitted, that the non-Western cultures had their own directions to follow till their course was forcibly cut off by the West?

The rationalist theory of history was indefensible. But it was enclosed within the pattern variables as a hidden assumption. In this guise it passed silently into the body of thought on modernization, which attempted to comprehend the Third World by means of Parsonian formulas.

Each pattern varied between the poles: traditional versus modern (rational). Each therefore classified role patterns and social structures not just as different but also as opposite. The analytic purpose was to define, as it was thought, the beginning point and end point of modernization. Identifying the cultures at the end point was easy—these were the industrialized societies of the West. But identification of both the preindustrial West and the nonindustrial Third World as the traditional, beginning phase rested on the unproven thesis of a rationalist direction to human history. It was, however, a convenient error. The modern West could be traced to its beginnings in its own past. Much more significant, its beginnings were seen in the past and contemporary Third World: was not the Third World today still living the Western past: or, at least, was it not in transition out of that past?

As a sort of fine tuning to the task of collapsing history into the Western frame, the pattern variables themselves underwent revision. They were transformed from dichotomies into continua by the interposition of transitional stages. Economies now had pretakeoff (traditional), takeoff (transitional), and mature (modern) stages—the series underdeveloped, developing, and developed suggested the same idea. Concomitantly, political culture had parochial, subject, and participant forms.

Gabriel Almond gives a rationale for this theoretical revision. He is speaking about the political order, but his remarks apply to the treatment of other institutions:

> The differences between Western and non-Western political systems have generally been exaggerated. This is in part due to the fact that the "limiting case" models of the Western system, on the one hand, and of the traditional and primitive systems, on the other, have been greatly overdrawn. The model of the Western system has over- stressed the functional specificity of political structure, while that of the traditional system has overstressed the undifferentiated and dif- fused character of political and social structure. [13]

Almond is arguing what he calls "the homogeneity of the universe of political systems." The political universe is homogeneous because all political systems are dualistic. As he says, "there are both primary and secondary structures in primitive and traditional political systems and the secondary structures have modern (specific, universalistic, and achievement) features."[14] And in the modern systems traditional structures persist. Consistent with assumptions of rationalist teleology, he calls the traditional structures "premodern."

However, from what he himself says, these traditional systems are not all of a piece. As defined here, structural dualism does not appear in the political order of Eskimo (Inuit) society, as is clear from his discussion. Among the Inuit, head man is the only politically differentiated role; and it functions intermittently, that is, on occasion as required. Even when specialized executive, legislative, and judicial structures have evolved, lineage groupings still perform occasional political functions. Intermittency, though, is not the same as dualism. It cannot be read as a sign of modernism lurking within band society or more complex systems. Nor are the specialized structures of the latter such a sign—surely not if they are part of kin-based societies. Only in "modernizing" societies as he calls them, does structural dualism in his sense appear in traditional polities; alongside traditional and intermittent structures there have now appeared governmental and political institutions with "specific, universalistic, and achievement features." Only these societies therefore merit the designation premodern.

These are also the only traditional societies that can accurately be described as in transition—indeed they were the ones that made the creation of a terminology of transition necessary. The terminology solved the problem of how to classify them. However, the more important question was, what set them in transition?

Gabriel Almond, again, and Sidney Verba give what would become the stock answer: cultural diffusion. According to them a knowledge of the processes of diffusion would even have led us to expect Western institutions to diffuse in the order they did: goods and their mode of production first; the infrastructure of modern economy next (transportation, communication, and education systems); modern organizational technology (bureaucracy); the formal trappings of democracy. The last diffuses only with the greatest difficulty. What they say on this matter encapsulates the mainstream view of the obstacles to modernization as a whole: "The second principal reason why the diffusion of democracy encounters difficulties among the new nations concerns the objective problems confronting these nations. They are entering history [*sic*] with archaic technologies and social systems."[15] As for the impetus behind their entry into "history," this is their own volition: "[They are] drawn toward the gleam and power of the technological and scientific revolutions."

The concept of diffusion was not nearly the answer. But to appeal to it revealed intrusion of the West as the historical agency of transition in the Third World, rather than an inner logic of history. Aspects of modernism that Westerners thought they perceived in the Third World past were artifacts of the contemporary Western presence. A theory of diffusion alone cannot clarify the real nature of this presence.

Frankly, it is gratuitous to suggest that the Third World was simply lured into modern society by the gleam of Western scientific-technological rationality and Western material wealth. That world, and the truth is known, was overwhelmed by Western colonialism, comprising a litany of human physical and cultural abuse. Colonialism, let it be said again, did not bring wealth to peoples of color. If, as the liberal interpretation insists, wealth was a lure, it had no more substance than that. It was not for nothing that Third World peoples were called the "wretched of the earth."

The Western god, rationality, also devoured its own communicants in wrenching contradictions. We know these as the social problems of our times. The table of contents of any reader on the problems of contemporary life would give a familiar list. One text, for instance, is a compendium of readings on inequality, racism, sexism, and institutions in crisis—the family, environment, workplace, education, health care, social services, criminal justice. [16] The list is an indicator of the seriousness of contemporary unhappiness. But it points only to the turmoil on the surface. More profoundly disturbing than the array of problems is a question arising out of the search for their origins: are they a product of the rationalist order itself, its rationalist values and the formal rationality of its institutions? Any one of the problems listed above could provoke this question as an unsettling suspicion, nevertheless open to possible rebuttal. Certain issues, however, posed it as unnerving certainty, none as starkly as the murderous violence of the modern West.

In *The Cunning of History,* Richard L. Rubenstein tells us that the twentieth century is marked by an "unprecedented magnitude of violence. . . . No century in human history can match the twentieth in the sheer number of human beings slaughtered as a direct consequence of the political activity of the great states. One estimate of the humanly inflicted deaths of the twentieth century places the total at about one hundred million. As fewer men have fallen prey to such natural ills as the plague and epidemics, the technology of human violence has taken up much of the slack. Those whom nature did not kill before their time were often slain by their fellow men." [17]

In the First World War about 6,000 men were killed every day for 1,500 days. The mountains of dead numbered ten million. At the Battle of Verdun, in a nine-month period, over 500,000 Frenchmen died resisting German attack on their national existence. The death toll among the German forces was approximately the same—and they, it must be noted, were not defending their national existence. This destruction produced no change in the battle lines. Equally for naught was the year-long Battle of the Somme where 410,000 British, 500,000 Germans, and 190,000 French perished. Rubenstein's main interest is not these grim statistics; his focus is rather on the more ominous meanings they have.

Mass death in our time had to await the maturing of certain

tendencies in Western culture. Critical was the creation of a technology of megaviolence, strange fruit of twentieth-century science. More fateful was what its unrestrained use in the terrible purpose of mass slaughter signified: the breaching of moral and political barriers that had long stood against such an eventuality. The bloody engagements at Verdun or at the Somme could not be written off merely as the inevitable union of war and death. "[Germany's General] Von Falkenhayn's strategy was biological. His objective at Verdun was to exterminate as many of the enemy as possible. . . . For the first time in memory a European nation had attempted to alter the biological rather than the political and military balance of power with an adversary."[18]

Rubenstein points to a phenomenon often observed, that among all species, population control mechanisms come into play when the balance between numbers and environmental resources is threatened. Could it be, he asks, that the German and Allied generals were in the silent grip of these forces when they presided over the destruction not only of enemy forces but of their own forces as well? He notes that despite the immigration of huge numbers of European men to the colonial outposts in Africa and Asia, the European population was still growing in the twentieth century.

Human beings, though, are not like lemmings mindlessly plunging into the ocean pursued by Malthusian specters. Attempts at population control like other human behaviors are culturally instituted, the relevant cultural features here being: definition of situations of material scarcity, definition of the unwanted, choice of an appropriate fate for such unfortunates, rationales for the choice, and moral-emotional responses to it. Cultures may be distinguished according to all of these elements and manifest their specific identities in terms of them. This considered, the carnage of the Great Wars is more an unmasking of the true face of Western culture and less, if at all, the tragic consequence of the hidden workings of some law of nature. In truth, it is the face of Western culture that Rubenstein wishes to paint. But, for the reasons just given and because of the details he himself justly emphasizes, his bow to Malthus (as the prophet of this law of population) must be differently situated within his sketch.

The Kung are an African hunter-gatherer people. Like other such peoples, they adjust numbers to resources by migrations of groups and by a constant flow of families into and out of the several bands that comprise the entire community, these movements being dictated by available food supplies. They also practice infanticide, the women exposing their children. It is an extreme solution and is not preferred, since as many children as possible are desired—both sexes equally. "It is my impression," says Lorna Marshall, ethnographer of the Kung, "that the Kung do not feel that they commit a crime or sin when they practise infanticide, but I believe that it is very disturbing to them nonetheless."[19] That they are disturbed is consistent with other aspects of their lifeways. Marshall tells us that they are practiced and dedicated in the avoidance of strife, and that she had never heard of a fight between bands, even from the very old people. " 'Fighting is very dangerous,' was the thought expressed by one of their headmen; 'someone might get killed.' " The key social feature which guarantees peace is the ethic of sharing. As with bands everywhere, such practices are institutionalized.

Band economy, of course, predates the Agricultural Revolution. The Kung therefore cannot exact more from nature; they remain subject to its generosity or its stringencies. Under these conditions the threat of absolute scarcity is real if occasional, and inexorably compels the extreme solution of infanticide from time to time. This is not the circumstance of cultures on the far side of plant and animal domestication. It certainly does not apply to the West, which lives at the center of the monstrous abundance of our times.

But is it possible, things being relative, that Europe, even with that productive capacity, was overpopulated at the time of the world wars? "It is doubtful whether there has ever been, in historical fact, an actual instance of the supposed Malthusian universal, of population overtaking agricultural productivity, multiplying right up to the limits of subsistence, and then being held in check by some new form of 'vice or misery' "—or, not to forget, war and human slaughter. This is the conclusion of Colin Clark after an investigation into rates of fertility and increase over millennia of hominid and human existence and into the contemporary period.[20]

Evidence from economies of both simple (primitive band) and complex (horticultural, agricultural, industrial) societies indicates, according to Clark, that the average woman gives birth to no more than six children during the child-bearing years. Population increase over 500,000 years (since *Homo erectus*) has not been due to an increase in this fertility but to other factors that have affected the rates of human mortality, such as increases in material productivity, the stability and security of the community, and, most important, improvement in medical knowledge. In the absence of these factors, which reduce mortality, the gross rate of six live births barely suffices to maintain population. As Clark notes, "primitive populations, generally speaking, do not increase." Since the conditions that limit survival in primitive life, poor medical knowledge especially, were widespread up to the seventeenth century, population growth up to this time was no more than .004 percent per annum. Only since the mid-nineteenth century, coincident with the worldwide dissemination of medical knowledge, have growth rates climbed to 1 percent, and more, annually.

But is there now a threat to resources, if not from fertility, then from greater survival? This too is fictitious. At Danish standards of cultivation and consumption (500 people per square mile), which Clark considers reasonable, the available 24 million square miles of cultivable land on the earth could support 12,000 million people, much more than the 2,300 million it maintained in 1963.

The exorcism of fertility as the demon element in the Malthusian scenario eliminates another one of those forces of nature— race and biology come to mind—often used to explain human behavior. The ground shifts and we look now to humanly instituted action, relevantly political and ideological choice. From this angle, fertility itself becomes an ideological construct.

Malthus feared not human fertility per se but the assumed fertility of the poorer classes, so given, in his assumption, to irresponsible and rampant sexual gratification. He ignored, and his intellectual descendants continue to ignore, the patent fact that the poor are politically barricaded in the economic hinterlands of national and international stratification systems, and the resources available there do not support their numbers. A program of redistribution would release them. This is what Clark proposes for the international context: free immigration, open markets, generous capital assistance to help poorer countries. It would also, consistent with observed trends in industrial society, lower their birthrates.[21]

Redistribution is an ancient economic practice that works. It extends band egalitarianism into so-called tribes, chiefdoms, and even states—a point I will extend later. But it requires a temper foreign to capitalist economy. Among some primitives, not to share essential resources is regarded as a sign of psychosis. The contrast with contemporary thinking is obvious. It is not the poor, I argue, who are to be feared but those who, with elegantly concealed malice, seek to keep them that way.

It is not only the poor who are endangered. They are part of a more numerous company—the mentally incompetent, the young in combat, those rendered stateless by war, and minorities are mentioned by Richard Rubenstein. They all have in common that they are politically impotent and many of them have suffered the ultimate injustice and are victims of state-instituted murder. Rubenstein calls them surplus populations. "It is important to note," he writes, "that the concept of a surplus population is not absolute. An underpopulated nation can have a redundant population, *if it is so organized* [my emphasis] that a segment of its able-bodied human resources cannot be utilized in any meaningful economic or social role."[22] The concept, observe, has shed its Malthusian origins (overpopulation as natural disaster). Rubenstein draws attention, in my view appropriately given what I have just said, to the politicoeconomic creation of population redundancy, to traditions and values that direct political action here, and to institutions that sustain political choice. His analysis underscores the central and indispensable role of bureaucracy in the mass death of the wars and, for the surplus living, in the rationally calculated miseries of living death.

The boast of modern bureaucracy, as we know, is an efficiency superior to what any other form of administration can deliver— it compares to other forms, said Weber, as the machine compares to nonmechanical modes of organization. The claim is real. Bureaucracy made possible the mass mobilization of the world wars, removing millions from their normal occupations, arming them, and dispatching them to the battle lines. But to what end?

"Both the British and the German generals made the same decision: Their country's young men were expendable."[23] The slaughter of these millions was thus foreseen, indeed anticipated. None of the commanders at the Somme or at Verdun was ever censured. And why should they have been? They were rationally efficient functionaries within the chain of command geared to the purposes of the bureaucratic state. What they did represented not their own decisions but decisions of those who held state power. And is it not true that Hitler understood that war gave an opportunity not presented in the normalcy of peacetime to rid Germany of groups he considered undesirables (that is, surplus)? After all, the creation and disposal of superfluous people, Rubenstein reminds us, began with the simple device of bureaucratic definition. Wartime simply extended the range of populations to be so considered.

The power of bureaucracy, its impact, and its purposes are not confined to war or to Nazi Germany. Some thinkers press the thesis that the social ills of peacetime originate from the bureaucratic order itself as its systemic products. Jerome Skolnick and Elliott Currie, for instance, explain that the readings in their text, cited earlier, take as their point of departure the structural rootedness of contemporary social problems in the institutions that govern American everyday life. In fact the selections show something more. "Problem" populations are not deficient in biology or in character structure, nor are they culturally disadvantaged and for these reasons dangerous, delinquent, and left out (nationally) or underdeveloped (internationally). They represent the failure of institutions to deliver the good life they promise to everybody. The major social problem is not people but the system in its normal functioning.

What then is the quality of normal life in America? A century ago Thoreau prophetically described it as one of quiet desperation. Philip Slater registers the following impression of America upon returning from abroad:

> Reentering America, one is struck first of all by the grim monotony of American facial expressions—hard, surly, and bitter—and by the aura of deprivation that informs them. . . . These perceptions are heightened by the contrast between the sullen faces of real people and the vision of happiness television offers: men and women ecstatically engaged in stereotyped symbols of fun—running through fields, strolling on beaches, dancing and singing. Smiling faces with chronically open mouths express their gratification with the manifold bounties offered by the culture. One begins to feel there is a severe gap between the fantasies Americans live by and the realities they live in. Americans know from an early age how they are supposed to look when happy and what they are supposed to do or buy to be happy. But for some reason their fantasies are unrealizable and leave them disappointed and embittered.[24]

Disillusioned and unfulfilled fantasies are merely a second-level disappointment, however. The deeper pain, says Slater, comes from the systemic and, for this reason, sustained frustration of some basic human needs by the American social order. These are, to paraphrase, the desire for community—trust and fraternity in collective life; the desire for engagement—for the chance, in other words, to confront directly (without the intermediation of red tape) problems in the social world, the source of which can be surely located in the environment; and the desire for dependence—to share with others the responsibility for control of impulse and the moral and purposive conduct of one's life.

The suppression of such needs is a given in the context of the competitive individualism of American life, an ethos radically hostile to collectivist principles. And yet individualism is indispensable (functional, in a certain parlance) to the social order. In economic life it is essential to geographical mobility of the work force and it legitimizes personal status seeking. It is at the foundation of interest-group politics (so-called democratic pluralism)—where in the hard political game are there tears for losers? ("I got mine," the saying goes. "Shame on you. You don't have yours.") And to enter the personal core, it is the basis of child-rearing practice as personal enterprise, the neolocal nuclear family (so easily mobile), and, of course, the romantic love complex. However injurious to the spirit, the bureaucratic order requires it. It is clear that, in this dispensation, pain is not a sanction for deviance; it is a normal outcome of conformity.

Within what I have called the personal core, there is a particularly bitter pathos to the disappointments of love and family life. In *Blue-Collar Marriage,* Mirra Komarovsky attempts to give us the flavor of life among America's working-class families—the majority population. The focal question is, how successful is the pursuit of happiness among America's majority? To this end the study explores many aspects of husband-wife-child(ren) relationships; the nature of relationships between the conjugal unit and external groups and institutions—consanguine and affinal kin, friends, voluntary groups, and entertainment complexes, formal organizations, and the economy; and the impact of these relationships on dynamics and quality of family life.

Komarovsky's study sample deliberately excluded troubled, delinquent, or disorganized couples, the usual target populations of studies of poorer families. It is a sample, in the terminology of the study, of stable families—those ordinary, mainstream white Americans who accept the goals of American life and pursue them by legitimate means. These are the men—and occasionally, in the given role structure, the women—who work.

The subjects are people marked by a commitment to rugged

economic self-help. They are also committed, both men and women, to the traditional sexual division of labor (this is 1962)—man as economic provider, woman as homemaker and, regardless of her moods and desires, sexual comforter (but not psychological intimate); and to the ideal of the neolocal household separate from families of origin. But their very conformity defeats many of them. Their normative goals remain elusive (economic self-sufficiency, the independent new household); or, when pursued (reticence, segregation of interests and leisuretime activities along sex lines), bring them misery. Economic failure is the hardest blow, and not only because of the marital deprivations it involves. It obstructs conjugal reciprocities, and its impact on the husband's self-image is devastating and progressive with age. Fully one-third of these families are less than moderately happy; 14 percent at least are very unhappy. "Life at its best is economically comfortable and rewarding, but for the great majority life is narrowly circumscribed."[25]

It adds to the tragedy that those trapped in these circumstances do not understand what forces put them there. They believe, as good Americans, that they are responsible for their fate. But their lives give the lie to this. They do not seek handouts from society. Their work histories show a migration from one low-paying job to another in an ambitious and determined attempt at self-betterment. But, mired in ideologies of self-recrimination, none of them could see what Komarovsky saw: "It seems to the author that society played a greater part in their unsatisfactory occupational status than the workers themselves were able to perceive . . . whatever their personal limitations, their schools and communities did not provide adequate guidance, training, and information."[26] Ignorance too is a penalty for conformity.

Lack of social insight compounds individual helplessness in the public realms. Insults, inconveniences, injuries are dispensed by minions uninvolved in their consequences. Their sources remain mysteriously hidden in opaque regions of impersonal bureaucratic authority. Their power to wound, all the more distant and unassailable for this reason, seems not merely capricious but malignant.

Such is the tone of life in the most developed outpost of bureaucratic paradise. The victims are the very votaries of rationalism. Is it any wonder that strangers have so little appeal against its efficient cruelties? And do they not become unwilling guinea pigs in organizational experiments that later crowd the nightmares of paradise itself? On this point let us consider some lessons from a major historical trauma of the twentieth century.

Incomprehensible brutality is not the only item in the legacy of horror bequeathed to our times by the genocide of the Jews. Richard Rubenstein subtitles his book *The Holocaust and the American Future*. He emphasizes that, pertinent to its own systemic creation—and reproduction—of human wastage among underprivileged ethnics of color and poor whites, America may find the Nazi invention of bureaucratically administered death and living death useful indeed. What requires attention, to follow his emphasis, is not the obvious aim of the death camps—the production of corpses—but the administrative intelligence that made them function. All major social institutions—production facilities, government bureaucracies, churches, medical organizations—had to be coordinated toward this end. [27]

America has not had death camps. But it did create the concentration camp (for the Japanese), the reservation (for native Americans), and that enclave of benign neglect, the black urban ghetto. Here, among these "surplus" living, the German lessons are particularly applicable: given a commitment to the demonic rationality inherent in modern systems of administration, total domination of unwanted populations is possible. The manner of this domination is a matter of record. Before they were sent to their final end the inmates of the death camps served all the purposes that could be invented by the deadly whims of power. The coldly calculated attrition of their life force induced by measured decreases in food over a predetermined period is a macabre illustration. The idea behind this experiment was to determine the minimum caloric intake needed for work. The subjects could be replaced from a limitless pool of victims. (In an earlier epoch, the same calculating rationality was evident. New England and British sea captains involved in the African slave trade worked with an accounting system that took stock of a precisely projected loss of their slave cargoes. "Some very respectable New England fortunes," says Rubenstein, "were made in those ventures.") If the fate of American minorities and poor white Americans does not replicate German experience, this is not because there is any less of a commitment in America to bureaucratic power and its consequences. (Here we should note, as Rubenstein does, that the capacity for administrative control via the retrieval of information has been exponentially enlarged since the Nazis by the development of computer technology.) It is simply that history repeats itself but does not do so exactly. Alongside the reservation and the ghetto there have appeared the white tenement and the urban village—all these on the fringes of life. But where else will necropolis appear?[28]

White Americans, and not just the working class, today still enjoy the false privilege of institutionalized racism. But Anglo techno-logic grips them just as coldly. Apart from its impersonally rendered indignities, this logic exposes them, *sine ira ac studio,* to a maiming, often lethal, technology. Writing in the context of the Vietnam War Philip Slater had this to say:

When all is said and done, American lives, while accorded an extraordinary value relative to those of Vietnamese civilians, still take a back seat relative to the death-dealing machinery they serve. Aircraft carriers, for example, are careless of human life even under the best of conditions, remote from the field of battle. Planes disappear under the sea with their pilots rather easily (the cost of planes lost through landing and takeoff accidents would have financed the poverty program), men are ignited by jet fuel, or devoured by jet engines, or run over by flight deck equipment, or blown into the sea by jet winds, or cut in half by arresting cables, or decapitated by helicopter blades. Even safety devices seem to be geared less to human needs than to the demands of the machinery: pilots ejected from F-4's regularly receive broken backs or other severe spinal injuries. The arguments about Viet Cong atrocities and saving American lives become ludicrous in the face of the daily reality of America's life-destroying technology.[29]

Yet, for all their pains, Americans enjoyed the license of genocidal scapegoating of the Vietnamese.

Slater is struck by the ferocity of American overkill in Vietnam: one thousand-to-one odds in firepower—machine-gunning helicopter pilots hosing peasants scurrying with rifles; smoke bombs and firebombs to flush targets from shelter; napalm and phosphorous bombs to incinerate them if they stay hidden; cluster bombs mowing fields with pellets, some with delayed-action fuses triggering later when those wandering by may be children or people going about their daily business; saturation bombing, noiseless from forty thousand feet, consuming square miles of jungle that suddenly explode into flames. American flyers sometimes saw their human targets. More often, Slater observes, they were engaged in mass killing from a distance.

Why create such an elaborate technology of extermination at a distance, he asks. And having created it, why put it to such unrestrained use? Other superpowers with equally destructive capabilities have not employed them. Is it that Americans, Slater suggests, enjoy the mass, impersonal slaughter of people who cannot retaliate because they themselves are victims of mass impersonal injuries from forces against which they are powerless? And is the indiscriminate destruction of the Vietnamese not consistent with the genocidal posture of Americans toward people of color in general—manifest, if any reminder is needed, in the destruction of North America's aboriginal peoples and cultures, the wasting abuse of black people, and the atomic devastation of Hiroshima and Nagasaki (the only instances of the use of nuclear devices against a population)? Genocide too, we should note, occurs at a distance, even though the victims are seen. Their humanity is hidden behind the subhuman identities imposed on them.

Bureaucratic genius is of course only a tool, though it does not simply orchestrate social ills. It creates some of them. (On this last, its specific contribution, since its many administrative forms penetrate society, is that it reinforces that impersonal lack of passion that corrodes human relationships in modern life and makes institutional compassion impossible.) But it does not generate the inequalities in the stratification system or the system itself, the victimization of the underprivileged, and ideologies that, as Parsons would say, maintain the boundaries of the social order—for instance, the belief in individual competence in the face of social-structural obstacles. The origins of these must be sought elsewhere within the rational order.

The derivation of the stratification system is straightforward. The modern system of classes derives from the modern economy. No more need be said concerning this.

To account for the inhumanities that accompany inequality is much more difficult; it is not simply a matter of analyzing the institutional fix that produces them. The question would remain, what value does a culture put on nature and life if it uses the might of its technical efficiency with such dismal consequences in personal life (Komarovsky), in daily living (Slater), and in the unusual circumstances of war (Rubenstein)? And why, despite the knowledge available from its rationalist investigations, has it maintained racial hostility and genocidal tendencies toward people of color? It is still useful, however, to discuss the institutional fix, as I call it, behind these realities, in particular the ideologies that legitimate stratification.

Stratification, functionalism tells us, is inevitable. It performs a set of tasks that must be performed in any society—allocating personnel to the total complex of roles within the division of labor, giving them access to materials and conveniences required to fulfill roles as expected, and rewarding them differentially according to the lesser or greater importance of roles for the social order. Because it is inevitable it is historically universal.

This theory does not imply the maltreatment of disadvantaged groups. But neither does it rule out its occurrence. Indeed, does it not legitimate maltreatment? One hopes for the best but expects the worst. If there is hope, this is not optimism. It is faith in eventual deliverance from social evil by technologic intelligence. But it is blind faith, which must explain social evil as contradicting the enlightened impulses for which rationalist culture praises itself. After all, how can reason produce such suffering, except unintentionally? And if inequality is a human given cannot the Western industrial order claim at least to have made the lot of the masses better? Is it not better to have displaced the extreme inequalities of ancient pyramidal structures with the opportunities for mobility offered by the diamond-shaped stratification systems of modern society? And from the perspective of rationalist teleology, what else is this but aspirations of humankind finding their fullest realization in the modern West? Their greater fulfillment then must await time.

Western history gives the lie to such a promise. Surely what we have seen in our time is not a drift toward the gradual elimination of suffering. Rather, it is clear that cruelty, even to the point of human devastation, has marched in step with the surging development of Western scientific and organizational genius. Can one say that this is not the fulfillment of a different promise?

> Weber's studies on bureaucracy and his related studies on Protestantism, capitalism, and disenchantment of the world are important in demonstrating how utterly mistaken is any view that would isolate Nazism and its supreme expression, bureaucratic mass murder and the bureaucratically administered society of total domination, from the mainstream of Western culture. . . . Nor ought we to be surprised that the bureaucratic objectivity of the Germans was paralleled by the diplomatic objectivity of the British. They were both nourished by the same culture. The culture that made the death camps possible was not only indigenous to the West but was an outcome, albeit unforeseen and unintended, of its fundamental religious traditions.[30]

In summary fashion Richard Rubenstein traces for us the dehumanized ethos of modern secular society from its biblical origins in the Judeo-Christian tradition. The Creator grants to Adam the right of dominion over the earth and Himself retreats from it to the supramundane celestial realms. This divine withdrawal secularizes nature and surrenders its treatment to humankind's discretion. But God remains present in the human order and politics must accord with His law. In time, in ancient Israel, the secularization of the political order begins, but divine judgment on things political is still rendered by the prophets. Thus the prophet Nathan condemns King David for his adulterous union with Bath-sheba and his murder of her husband. And in that world King David knew he was not beyond divine sanction. Now it has come to pass that God is no longer present in the modern political order and there are no prophets to thunder his injunctions. The law that governs is the law of a new omnipotent entity with the supreme power of life and death, the modern secular state, which answers only to the dictates of formal reason. Rubenstein's assessment of these developments bears repeating: they do not represent a negation of biblical religion but rather its cultural fulfillment.

Religion, they say, enshrines ultimate values. Protestant Christianity, notably Calvinism, preached that the division of humankind into the elect and the damned was hallowed by divine decree. Science, secular pretender-surrogate of divine revelation, confirms this dispensation. Social process then has only made real what God and science have ordained, however much liberal sentimentality may cringe over its cruel excesses.[31]

The obverse image of sentimentality is pessimism, emotionally of course and, more to the point here, intellectually. For the intellect must yield to convenience and thus abrogate its responsibility and power to enlighten. Weber is revered as the most insightful prophet of the rationalist course of history. But among those that revere him, who senses his irony, a power of perception indeed that can come only to those who see this course of history, without illusion, as it is and what grimly it promises to be? Against the effort wasted in contemporary intellectual celebration of the West stands Weber's assessment, carrying the weight of his authoritative analyses:

No one knows who will live in this cage in the future, or whether at the end of this tremendous development entirely new prophets will arise, or there will be a great rebirth of old ideas and ideals, or, if neither, mechanized petrification, embellished with a sort of convulsive self-importance. For of the last stage of this cultural development it might well be truly said: "Specialists without spirit, sensualists without heart," this nullity imagines that it has attained a level of civilisation never before achieved. [32]

The liberal temper today has not been faithful to the principled rigor of its most important mentor. Seduced by privilege it has lost its way in the storms of cruelty released by the system it worships. Hence it attributes to other cultures the serious delicts of its own. This may not be the intended consequence of the theses of the historical inevitability of stratification and the rationalist direction in universal history, but it is always implied here.

The functionalist theory of stratification and the rationalist theory of history, observe, are cultural arguments. But they protect privilege and defend oppression, however indirectly—purposes once served by biological and racial determinisms. In a grave intellectual regression, they can now, for instance, be used to explain Third World poverty, nationally in America or internationally, as the result not of racial inferiority but of cultural inadequacy. But then, ultimately—since cultural practices have remarkable inertia and always seem to be the natural, that is, the biologically rooted, way of doing things—culture and biology must imperceptibly merge in the mind as identities. And certainly the mind cannot help but see that Third World cultures are borne by races of color, the "inferior" races in the paradigm of an earlier era. And if they left nothing for history, how can their cultures, which are today still in the anteroom of rationalist development, do so? By this route, and no doubt by others, liberal thought lost the usefulness of the insights of cultural analysis, one of the most important bodies of ideas in its tradition.

The iron cage is here. Insight is needed now more than ever.

But its sources lie outside the boundaries of Western experience. Except from prophets crying in the wilderness without influence, has anyone ever heard of a strategy of development for the West, for America, that is informed by, shall we say, substantive rationality? It is an effect of living in the cage of Western intellect that the visionary impulse has withered, deprived of the nourishment it needs from universal history, which is culturally pluralistic.

Liberals, of course, admit cultural pluralism—did Boas not point the way? But their bow in this direction, especially in American liberal thought, has the yawning emptiness of protocol. Below the surface of formalism run the powerful currents of their ethnocentric hatreds of other cultures and peoples of color that bear them—none so virulent as the hatred of blacks and their history.

The mistaken historical notions of liberal mainstream thought, as I have described them here, could be challenged on the grounds of their racist principles and practices. Indeed, to set the historical record straight required that I begin with such a challenge. From within the Western tradition itself, socialist humanism and revolutionary Marxism sought to overturn the liberal vision of history. Socialist humanism, one would think, surely stood against racism and for cultural tolerance, and could resurrect black history (which has a very special place in Europe's encounter with the Third World) from the crypts of Western distaste. Or, for these purposes, was humanism less illuminating a vantage point than it was thought to be? This is the question to be answered next.

2

WHAT ABOUT THE
RADICAL ALTERNATIVE?

Do Marx and Marxism correct the liberal misinterpretations of Third World histories, European culture, and universal history as discussed in the first chapter? In this chapter I will attempt to answer that question, beginning with an excursus that explains the theoretical strengths and distinctiveness as a body of social thought that Marxism might claim for itself, and that puts the Marxian tradition in perspective of the argument.

It is true that modern sociology ultimately derived its classification of cultures and world history from Hegel. In its beginnings though, sociology had established its identity and claim as the science of social relations in society on the basis of an antiphilosophical stance. More exactly, it disclaimed transcendentalism. If it was "philosophical" at all this was "by virtue of its general positivistic character."[1] It was thus consistent that nascent sociology ignored other concepts central to Hegel's analysis of history and society—the notion and the dialectic. In the new science these seemed unscientific.

For Hegel, to repeat what may be familiar, the notion of a thing differed from the thing as it appeared in reality. The notion indicated how far from its true identity (self, essence) a thing in its appearance(s) was. It showed what a thing would or could be.

With respect to society it showed its destiny. Strictly speaking, as Herbert Marcuse argues, this was not teleology since the notion here indicated what society ought to become.

In becoming, a thing went beyond, obliterated its many appearances in reality. This process is the dialectic. It says that identity is a process of going beyond (resolving) self-generated contradictions. In general, in the inorganic and organic realms, the contradictions are nonantagonistic: they are ontological changes. In society, however, the contradictions are not ontological; they are social. And in hierarchical systems they are antagonistic.

The question is, what will the resolution of conflict produce? What is the notion that society ought to fulfill? Human destiny, said Hegel, is a society of Freedom, Justice, and Right. These concepts have a metaphysical, transcendental aspect. If, as positivist sociology would claim, they cannot be empirically measured, they are indeed unscientific. However, they are not completely transcendental. Hegel himself describes the concrete manifestation of Freedom.

Freedom, Justice, and Right are fulfilled where the person of the individual is protected by inalienable rights before the law; where all are guaranteed access to ownership of property; where the state (preferably, but not only, a constitutional monarchy) stands above the fray of civil competition with Absolute Power, but is bound by constitutional law and has as its prime purpose the full development of the individual. Omit the Absolute State and one has the constitutional blueprint of the liberal democracies today.

In fact, the difficulty with Hegel was not his "unscientific" metaphysics. Clearly the transcendental could be made measurable. But to adopt the Hegelian concept of notion, even with a liberal redefinition, would invalidate the boast that liberal society was the just order of human strivings come into reality. And to accept the dialectic as the motor of history meant admitting that the historical present, a scene of many antagonistic

hierarchies, must too pass away in cataclysms of social struggles. Liberal thought, however, which had witnessed (and cham-
pioned) the constitutional guarantees of an active role for the
masses in the political economy of modern capitalism, held fast
to a different proclamation. In the conventional wisdom, the
popular vote and the right to labor organization and pressure-
group politics had ushered in postindustrial society, the end of
ideology. Effectively that was construed as the end of history.

But is there really nothing beyond the bureaucratic end of the
world? Does human fate finally come to rest in the hands of those
"specialists without spirit" and "sensualists without heart" that
Max Weber described?

It is remarkable that these questions could be posed by the
very intellect whose historical investigations provide the most
firmly grounded underpinnings for the ahistorical conclusions
of modern liberal sociology. Weber's work is a massive cross-
cultural ethnography of human societies in history. On a theoretical level it permits what might be called empirical general-
ization on certain institutional relations within systems; and,
as concerns cross-cultural comparisons, on certain institutional
properties and features of social systems. For all its empirical
wealth no measure of the ideal Perfection of a system, and all it
says about history as dynamic, can be generated from it. The
truth is that Weber, unlike his descendants, is not drawing his
own conclusions (presented as ironic questions) solely within
the limits allowed by his empirical observations. Indeed, if one
keeps these limits in mind, one notes that his conclusions are
theoretically unwarranted. It is a different matter, however, outside those limits—in that realm defined by substantive rationality.

Substantive rationality is the Weberian equivalent of the Hegelian notion. It retains the notion as an integral part of any
social analytic schema. Doubtless, "the concept . . . is full of
difficulties." Nonetheless, "it is necessary *to take account of the fact
that economic activity is oriented to ultimate ends of some kind* [my

emphasis], whether they be ethical, political, utilitarian, hedonistic, the attainment of social distinction, of social equality, or of anything else."[2]

There are many ultimate ends. But, however diverse they are, they all represent "the degree in which a given group of persons, no matter how it is delimited, is or could be adequately provided with goods by means of an economically oriented course of social action."[3] These ends determine, and allow, judgments concerning the distribution of the social wealth. Whatever the image of distribution in other cultures, in the Western tradition social justice has always called for an egalitarian, or more egalitarian, distribution of the social product. Weber's judgments on modern bourgeois society, therefore, do not arise merely from his own ethical whims. He is speaking from tradition.

The term *objectivity,* when applied to Weber's work, is usually made to refer to his unimpassioned empiricism uncontaminated, as it is thought, by value judgment. Here, I am arguing that his objectivity, in this sense, is preliminary to his judgment, and that this judgment is equally objective. Further, his analysis, any analysis, would be incomplete without judgment; and would be less objective for being so. It follows that if he could dare to imagine a world beyond the "tremendous development" of the bourgeois present, this act of imagination is objectively defensible and theoretically necessary.

What will this world be? We are not told. New prophets? A rebirth of old ideas and ideals? It is significant that the few images of an unclear future are drawn from the past, and not from any potential hidden in the present. But if the present holds no promise, it is also true that prophecy is gone. And the Western past never solved injustice.

It would seem that Weber left for his descendants more than they intellectually digested. By making substantive rationality a formal part of analysis he left social thought precisely with the burden of thinking beyond the present since this is what objective analysis indicates. Social thought, so to speak, should have assumed the mantle of prophecy—a new mode of prophecy armed with modern tools of investigation.

Contemporary mainstream sociology, however, disassembled Weber's analytic schema into its "formal" and "substantive" parts and omitted the latter from its paradigms. Hence, conventional sociology could not critically—from the substantive-ethical point of view—address the present; examine, or reexamine, the past with insight; or, least of all, imagine a future outside the contemporary order. Sociologists, of course, are free to state and follow their personal ethical beliefs in criticizing the social order and proposing reformist or revolutionary changes. But their science does not lend its authority to giving ethical choices an analytic role in their thinking. By self-definition, this science cannot do so.

Against this background, Marxism and historical materialism, as currents of thought opposed to the liberal viewpoint, have a specific significance. They unite scientific method, substantive reasoning, and programmatic historical vision in a single analytic package. This is no surprise since they explicitly acknowledge their Hegelian origins.

For Marx, the end of the dialectic was not Freedom (Self-Consciousness), but the destruction of exploitative relations. He identified the tensions in the modern age as the class antagonisms peculiar to contemporary society. He preserved Hegel's idea that what exists is not what ought to be—because it was not substantively reasonable. And he showed which specific social conflicts had to be resolved in order to give rise to a nonexploitative system.

Although he was indebted to Hegelianism, Marx revised it—putting it, as he said, on its feet. He defended his revisionist claim because of the role he assigned to class struggle in the Marxian system. The class struggle explains that the worldview of a nonexploitative society, or any worldview, will become the worldview of the new age when the class bearing a given worldview (the workers) ascends to power, as it is destined by its circumstance to do. Idea systems, in other words, do not simply shrivel from internal decay or come to flower in the social consciousness because of their compelling beauty, humanitarianism, truth, or whatever else. To those causes one must add the idea of worker's power, a formulation that went far beyond Hegel's distrust of working people in the political arena. And if Hegel felt that the Prussia of his time was the terminus of history, Marx felt no such thing about his own present.

It is evident that, from the Marxian perspective, liberal thought, itself a product of forces that brought liberal society into being, is as historical and temporal as any other worldview. This mutability is simply the fate of ideas that stand in the service of substantively irrational systems. It also results from the fact that as a general rule social relations and ideas change as the forces of production in society change and explode them. The first idea can be demonstrated through an exercise in Marxist political economy. The second is a task for materialist evolutionism. In materialist evolutionism we also encounter the Marxian view of non-Western cultures in history.

We recall that mainstream sociology binds the Third World into what I call a rationalist interpretation of history: Third World cultures mirror the Western past; and the Western present is the final development of the drive to rationality that is germinally present in all cultures—hence its claim to historical permanence. As I argued earlier, this interpretation is a piece of intellectual sorcery that magically eliminates European colonialism as the cause of any apparent rationalist motion in Third World histories. In the rationalist theory the Third World is juxtaposed to Europe; in historical fact the Third World was gobbled up and wrenched out of autonomous development by the West.

Clearly, how adequate an answer is to this interpretation depends on the meaning it assigns to colonialism in Third World histories. It also depends on how the theory views the Third World before European contact. On both measures the Marxian view of history is wanting. It is particularly deficient on the first.

Further, errors in the theory have had pernicious consequences in Marxist missionizing practices among Third World peoples.

Let us consider Marx on colonialism. Shlomo Avineri offers the following comment: "Since Marx postulates the ultimate victory of socialism on the prior universalization of capitalism, he necessarily arrives at the position of having to endorse European colonial expansion as a brutal but necessary step toward the victory of socialism . . . the horrors of colonialism are dialectically necessary for the world revolution of the proletariat since without them the countries of Asia (and presumably also Africa) will not be able to emancipate themselves from their stagnant backwardness." He adds: "Marx's views on imperialism can be painfully embarrassing to the orthodox communist."[4]

Marx arrived at this indefensible moral position because of an intellectual misstep and, behind that, a Eurocentric world vision and system of values. Both misstep and Eurocentrism are captured in the phrase "stagnant backwardness." This is Avineri's rendering of Marx's own descriptions of social formations in the non-European world: "barbarian and semibarbarian countries," "nations of peasants," "Asiatic mode of production," "oriental despotism"—these terms all designate, for Marx, cultures that have no history. The question is, how could Marx have come to this conclusion given that he knew enough about non-Western society, in India if not Africa, to have decided differently? The answer lies in what he discovered about the dynamics of European cultural change and what, consequently, he came to expect about sociocultural dynamics in general.

Beyond the stage of primitive communalism (savagery and barbarism), as Marx and Engels tell it, lie the epochs of class struggles that define history from this point and the different forms of civil society within which they occur. These forms are evolutionary. "In broad outlines," says Marx, "Asiatic, ancient, feudal, and modern bourgeois modes of production can be designated as progressive epochs in the economic formation of society."[5] Since he is trying to reconstruct the historical passage to modern capitalism, they are also progressive epochs in the rise of individualism (particularly in its aspect as the pursuit of self-interest and personal gain), private property, and "the separation of free labor from the objective conditions of its realization—from the means and material of labor,"[6] that is, the rise of a free labor market.

However, while it is true, for Marx, that the feudal mode evolves out of the ancient and gives rise to the modern bourgeois, which in its turn will explode into socialism, the Asiatic mode did not generate ancient slave society—or any other subsequent form. In fact, this appears as a puzzling exception to the Marxian law of historical motion, and of course to Marx himself. Unlike other systems, it does not seem that the Asiatic system will perish when "the productive forces for which there is room in it have developed"; and "new higher relations of production" are not waiting for "the material conditions of their existence" to mature in *its* womb. Indeed Marx observed that it had been enduringly repetitive: the oriental commune, the Indian village as the one example, had survived the "majestic ruin" of super-structures that had occurred periodically throughout oriental history.

What was the source of this stability, or as Marx would say, "this undignified, stagnatory, and vegetative life . . . this passive sort of existence?"[7] The query itself indicates how different he thought oriental society was, since the question he posed about the other formations was, what made them *move*—specifically, what made them move toward capitalism? Answers to these questions he discovered and provided himself.

"Once men finally settle down," he says, there emerge both the tribal community—a modification of the earlier human community based on collectivist principles, which is due to be further modified by the circumstances of settled life—and communal property on which it is based. There are, however, different forms of communal property. *Pre-capitalist Economic Formations* seeks to determine which of these forms has the structural potential to force the development of capital and free labor.

The Asiatic—and the African—as noted, is the form most

resistant to change. Both in the primitive stage and after state-hood, there is little or no room for individuation: it is the commune that owns the land while the individual, as a member of the commune, is entitled to what Marx calls possession, which is to say, use. The individual therefore does not develop in opposition or contradistinction to the community. "He is firmly rooted [within it] as a generic being, a tribal being, a herd animal."[8]

Further, the village commune is based on the "unity of agriculture and craft manufacture" so that "the circle of production is self-sustaining."[9] Hence, as distinct from the European experience, the division of agricultural and nonagricultural labor does not appear in opposed, or even distinct, locations, such as country and town. As a consequence—this we must infer—there is no living space (townships) that can harbor a merchant class surviving in the interstices, so to speak, of village society, accumulating monetary wealth and waiting to purchase labor (dispossessed from agriculture and handicraft) and instruments of labor to unite them in a new mode of production, manufacture of commodities, that will destroy the old communal system. The conclusion suggests itself that if labor is set loose from the commune by any disturbance it must ultimately return to village life since indeed this is the only life that exists.

Here we must ask, where can disturbance originate? There is, for one thing, population expansion. We can take it that this will be absorbed into village life. Marx also rules out a classic source of instability, class conflict based on the antagonism of the propertied and the propertyless. This cannot be generated internally since the individual, to repeat, is firmly rooted as a communal member and has no property to lose. Nor can it come about through the imposition of slavery or serfdom on alien tribes. As Marx explains, "in the self-sustaining unity of manufactures and agriculture . . . conquest is not so essential a condition as where landed property, agriculture, predominate exclusively."[10]

I shall return to the nonexpansionist character of oriental society. For the moment, it is possible to derive the following conclusions. Whatever the contradictions in oriental socioeconomic structures may be, they do not include class antagonisms. Nor do they result in the kind of linear historical development that marks European culture—the unfolding of individualism, private property, free labor, and capital. If anything, they generate a cyclical, repetitive history. Concerning this cycle Marx observes that it does not rupture from the inside. Speaking of the loss of property, a critical element in the rise of wage-labor, he states: "In the oriental form this loss is hardly possible, *except as a result of entirely external influences* [my emphasis]."[11] European colonialism, he knew, was one such "external influence."

Obviously Marx was aware that the structural tensions, which are precisely the ones that move European history, are absent from oriental society. Comparing Europe and the Orient on this measure, he could simply have considered them different—unrelated sociocultural accidents on "the great arc of potential human purposes and motivations," as Ruth Benedict would say. Even Marx's genius, needless to say—and in any case it has already been said—was limited by assumptions of humanity and history current during his time, so that for him Europe remained the measure of comparison. It would have been easier to drop these assumptions and see Europe and the Orient as noncomparable, except formally, if he had been able to see that they were different over the entire course of their (separate) histories.

"We may take it for granted," he says, "that pastoralism, or more generally a migratory life, is the first form of maintaining existence."[12] It is implied here that the transition from a migratory life—which Marx, note, identifies only with pastoralism—is historically universal. Engels, in *The Origin of the Family, Private Property, and the State* (written on the basis of notes left by Marx), advances the thesis of another, more famous, universal transition—the transition from matriarchy to patriarchy. If these claims were true, Marx (and Engels) could assume that historical development had been driven by structural impulses common to all cultures. It could then be said that Europe and the non-European world had had comparable histories in the ancient past. And, different as they were in structure since those transitions, both were similarly systems based on "the exploitation of man by man." Both could be equally expected to witness the revolutionary restoration of communal society under the same forces, it could be assumed, as had operated in the past. The peculiar cyclical history of Asiatic society would mean that this form was more rather than less resistant to change but not completely so. The external shock of European colonialism, in this view, merely hastened an inevitable process.

The horrors of modern imperialism would give birth to a new communalism. Even this new era was cast in the image of Europe. It depended on the industrial base that capitalism provided, but with the transformation of the raison d'être of capitalist production. It would be communalism at a higher level, so to speak, allowing a fuller development of the individual than was possible under the pristine form. Marx paints the bright picture of this new time by way of contrast with ancient society and by a redefinition of the meaning of industrial abundance in the age to come:

> Among the ancients we discover no single enquiry as to which form of landed property, etc., is the most productive, which creates maximum wealth. Wealth does not appear as the aim of production. . . . The enquiry is always about what kind of property creates the best citizens. . . .
>
> Thus the ancient conception, in which man always appears (in however narrowly national, religious or political a definition) as the aim of production, seems much more exalted than the modern world, in which production is the aim of man and wealth the aim of production. In fact, however, when the narrow bourgeois form has been peeled away, what is wealth, if not the universality of needs, capacities, enjoyments, productive powers, etc., of individuals, produced in universal exchange? What, if not the full development of human control over the forces of nature—those of his own nature as well as those of so-called "nature"? What, if not the absolute elaboration of his creative dispositions, without any preconditions other than antecedent historical evolution which makes the totality of this evolution—i.e., the evolution of all human powers as such, unmeasured by any *previously established* yardstick—an end in itself?

What is this, if not a situation where man does not seek to remain something formed by the past, but is in the absolute movement of becoming? In bourgeois political economy . . . this complete elaboration of what lies within man appears as the total alienation and the destruction of all fixed, one-sided purposes; as the sacrifice of the end in itself to a wholly external compulsion. Hence in one way the childlike world of the ancients appears to be superior; and this is so, in so far as we seek for closed shape, form and established limitation. The ancients provide a narrow satisfaction, whereas the modern world leaves us unsatisfied, or, where it appears to be satisfied with itself, is *vulgar* and *mean*. [13]

This is a humanist ideal for the world. A human(ist) universal is constructed from European values, particularly the passionately aggressive materialist urges of this culture, and its preoccupation with a type of individual development unfettered by history and tradition—a preoccupation expressed in our day by the saying, "the sky's the limit." Human perfectibility, even of the spirit, is anchored in materialistic acquisitiveness. Note also that acquisitiveness, unlike the body appetites, is in its nature unbounded. Only culture can define the point of its satiation. Where, as in the modern world, this is not given "closed shape, form and established limitation" it wanders over anomic terrain created by the fantasies of imagination, the feverish drive of individualistic ambitions, and the whims of bureaucratic systems that claim almighty power. We understand why, among moderns, future orientation has the status of a virtue.

Marx knew that modern capitalism was, as he said, "vulgar and mean." But he was European. He chose to see promise in industrial power and hope for a communal industrial future. And he saw Indian communalism—as he would have seen African socialism—as vegetative, stagnant. This was not racial distaste. He did not admire the ancient Slavonic and Russian systems either; and the phrase, "the idiocy of rural life," aptly described what was, for him, the backwaters of European society. His assessment rested on the historical research he did and on a conception of laws of historical motion emerging from his investigations. What I have called an intellectual misstep is the (mis)application of his historical conclusions to non-European systems. The epithet, stagnant, is the result of this misstep.

As noted, Marx's errors in historical analysis did not derive from racial bigotry. But they were redefined to this end by modern-day prophets of workers' power in the name of—could anything be more ironic?—proletarian othodoxy.

Proletarian and wage-earning classes existed worldwide because capitalism existed worldwide. But the face of capitalist oppression was not the same everywhere. There were different class oppressions resulting from the varying degrees of capitalist modernization of the economy in different countries; or from the impact of different precapitalist cultural traditions on the shape of modern life—thinking in these instances only about European countries. Capitalism originated or restructured sexual antagonisms, again differently in different places. Very much to the point here, capitalist oppression was also racial. In the circumstances, what could proletarian orthodoxy mean? What was the correct thinking and what was the correct strategy for revolution?

"Isn't our struggle a struggle of ideas?" asked the Spanish tourist. "Doesn't it involve your head?"

"It involves my head, of course, but not my eyes," the painter explained with a smile.

"In other words," he added, "I'd like to go on seeing things with my own eyes." . . .

"In our era all roads lead to Communism," said the Spanish tourist, to restore harmony among his comrades. "But we can't all be Communists in the same way."

"I've staked my life on the Proletarian Revolution," explained the painter. "If I haven't staked my eyes as well, it's only to reserve myself the right of seeing what happens to my life."

". . . I'm taking part, not only as a gambler, but as a player too; as a player who is entirely wrapped up in the game and has staked himself. Entirely, I say, except for the eyes."

"I don't understand," declared the dentist.

"In short, I refuse to blindfold myself," the painter concluded. "I'll do absolutely everything you expect me to do, but with my eyes open."[14]

"The committee has decided against such demonstrations," Brother Jack said. "Such methods are no longer effective." . . .

"Such crowds are only our raw materials, one of the raw materials to be shaped to our program."

I looked around the table and shook my head. "No wonder they insult me and accuse us of betraying them. . . ."

"Very well, so now hear this: We do not shape our policies to the mistaken and infantile notions of the man in the street. Our job is not to ask them what they think but to *tell* them!"

"You've said that," I said, "and that's one thing you can tell them yourself. Who are you, anyway, the great white father?"

"Not their father, their leader. And your leader. And don't you forget it."

"*My* leader sure, but what's your exact relationship to them?"

His red head bristled. "The leader. As leader of the Brotherhood, I am their leader."

"But are you sure you aren't their great white father?" I said, watching him closely, aware of the hot silence and feeling tension race from my toes to my legs as I drew my feet quickly beneath me. "Wouldn't it be better if they called you Marse Jack?" . . .

And I spun my chair half around on its hind legs as he came between me and the light, gripping the edge of the table, spluttering and lapsing into a foreign language, choking and coughing and shaking his head as I balanced on my toes now, set to propel myself forward . . . as suddenly something seemed to erupt out of his face. You're seeing things, I thought . . . as his arm shot out and snatched an object the size of a large marble and dropped it, plop! into his glass . . . and there on the bottom of the glass lay an eye. A glass eye. A buttermilk white eye distorted by the light rays. . . .

". . . You must accept discipline. Either you accept decisions or you get out. . . ."

I stared into his face, feeling a sense of outrage.[15]

Orthodoxy in revolutionary practice was thus defined by Russian bolshevism through the agency of the Comintern. Everywhere in Europe and in Third World countries the conspiratorial, underground style in organization became de rigueur for communist revolutionaries. This style derived from the historical experience of the Bolsheviks in Russia, where cultural tradition had never granted legitimacy to political opposition. In the many theaters of political struggle, policy changed not in creative response to changes in local circumstances, but as dictated by an ever-changing Russian party line that swerved with international balance-of-power politics in which the Soviet system was involved as a world power. The survival interests of the Soviet state on the world stage overshadowed and overwhelmed local interests. Thus, in Ellison, for example, the Russian eye could see better from that great distance what the eye of the local Brotherhood could not see at its own feet. So great was the prestige of the Russian Revolution; and so profound was the hope felt by millions, as Richard Crossman says, "that Russia was on the side of the workers."[16]

Communists claimed to have the only true revolutionary faith and practice (the party line of the moment). This generated among themselves incessant and bitter wranglings over left or right deviations, intolerant attacks on the integrity of those suspected of doctrinal lapses, ostracisms, and expulsions. And it led to a wretchedly unprincipled manipulation, subversion, and betrayal of allied organizations that held to different ideologies whether liberal, left, or nationalist. In dealings with nationalities and ethnics of color, political-intellectual intolerance and racial intolerance coincided. This was not meant to be obvious; but where white communists met black Americans, Africans, and West Indians it could hardly be concealed.

It must be said, however, that while bolshevism is to be blamed for falsely claiming revolutionary political omniscience and for defining the direction of the struggles of oppressed peoples worldwide to serve Soviet state interests (the destruction of Western imperialism), it was not directly responsible for the racism of American and European communists. George Padmore offers testimony on this question. Padmore, a Trinidadian, made the freedom and independence of colored peoples and Africans his life's work, and he enjoys the stature of being one of the principal architects of Pan-Africanism. He was made a colonel in the Red Army and was later head of the African bureau of the Comintern. He sought to use the resources and inspiration of the Russian Revolution to the end of Pan-African liberation until he became convinced that Africans were pawns in a world-embracing strategy for Soviet survival. He then broke with Russian-inspired communism.

Padmore gives great praise to Lenin's radical departure from orthodox Marxism in his appeal beyond the Russian industrialized workers (a small number within the total population) to the peasantries and the non-Russian nationalities subject within the czarist empire: "Lenin's party alone among the anti-aristocracy organizations which participated in the revolutionary upheaval, took a firm, uncompromising position on the question of national freedom and self-determination, which found response in the ambitions and aspirations of the subject nationalities and racial minorities living under Czarist rule."[17]

Without the peasants and the non-Russian nationalities—and this was admitted by Stalin—the Revolution could not have succeeded. Subsequently such unorthodox alliances, which had emerged accidentally as tactical pragmatism, became enshrined as strategy on the National and Colonial Question for communist parties in the West. In principle and in fact the Soviet state committed itself to the nationalist anticolonial struggles of all oppressed races.

It is true that the Kremlin bears the responsibility for manipulating these struggles to stay within the rigidities of the Russian party line, but it did not confound political convenience with racial preference. On the whole, according to Padmore, the Soviet leadership held no truck with the color bar.[18] Unfortunately, the same could not be said of the communist brethren in Europe and America.

In *The Crisis of the Negro Intellectual*, Harold Cruse makes the important criticism of American communists, white and black,

that they never Americanized Marxism. The official party line
was proletarian unity. It ignored the reality of European eth-
nicities within the party: Jewish, Russian, Latvian, Polish, and
Finnish socialist groupings, to mention a few of these, antedated
the birth of the American Communist Party; and these groups
entered the party with their ethnic identities intact. The party
line also ignored the historic reality of white over black. Indeed,
to be frank, the first choice made it easy to rationalize the second—certainly a desperate convenience for white Marxists.

What direction could the Americanization of Marxism have
taken from the time of the entry of communism into American
political life? Cruse mentions that there were few instances of
original thinking and insight that could stand as creative revi-
sions to Marxism on this question throughout the life of the
American Communist Party. He mentions one George Halonen,
who belonged to one of the foreign (European) language socialist
groups. In a January 1926 issue of *The Workers Monthly*, he urged
that the party support the economic cooperative movements created by the socialist federations to support their economic, social, political, and cultural group interests. For him, they were
authentic communist activity—as authentic as the interethnic
and interracial trade unionism that the party was then insisting
upon as the correct organizational tool for the struggle of a
united working class.[19]

Not only were the federations and cooperatives working class
in origin, they precisely extended the reach of Marxist practice to
the peculiar American situation of a culturally plural society
where social advancement occurs as a result of ethnic identity,
solidarity, and organization. The cooperative movement had
sprung up to confront Anglo-Saxon dominance in American institutional life including, as it came to pass, the Communist
party. Cruse writes: "These Socialist federations were able to
wield enormous political and financial power both in the Communist Party and in Moscow precisely because they were based
on the cooperative method of economic group development."[20]

Halonen's novel suggestions on Marxist practice received

theoretical grounding a few years later from V. F. Calverton, founder-editor of *Modern Quarterly*. Calverton was an independent communist, as was his journal.[21] In the March 1931 issue of *American Journal of Sociology* he discussed a notion he had been thinking of for some time—cultural compulsives. The term refers to the entire complex of cultural forces that shape individual behavior and thought. In another article in *Modern Quarterly* he argued that cultural compulsives shape individual styles of literary criticism—as well as styles of morality, politics, education, and economics. A literary judgment then was culturally bound. It could claim to be absolute only by being so instituted against other contending judgments that were equally culture-bound. Clearly, the logic of the concept could easily explain Anglo-Saxon dominance in the party leadership; and later, Jewish dominance in defining party theory and practice for the European language groups—and for black people.

In the early 1920s the federations were incorporated into the party as sections and relieved of their wide-ranging group functions. And black communists never followed Calverton's line of thinking. These developments killed the threat that such thinking might be applied to understanding and criticizing Jewish direction of communist strategy for blacks in America.

Jews became the party theoreticians in the thirties following the earlier Anglo-Saxon period in the twenties. According to Cruse, this earlier period saw a more flexible and open-ended inquiry on the question of blacks and a greater willingness to debate the issue than was true under Jewish ascendancy. When party organization became more rigid black communists religiously took their cues from the party line. "What should have been the Negro theoreticians' period of pioneering achievements and creative originality became, by default, a period of cheap militancy, imitative posturing, and a blind evasion of Negro realities."[22] Blacks followed the line; but the Jewish leadership mapped the course, posed the questions, and provided the answers.

To speak for blacks Jews had to master, or at least claim that they had mastered, black cultural compulsives. The result was publications and statements on the black question that claimed to be more authoritative than what blacks had to say about themselves. The authority of party pronouncements was leveled particularly against any claims to national identity that blacks might make. The supportive assumption here was that Marxism was a white social science that had to be taught to blacks, much as whites had to teach them democracy. Cruse tells the story that during a black-white inner-party conflict in Harlem between 1949 and 1951 some whites heatedly remarked: "It was white people who brought the ideas of Marxism to Harlem in the first place."[23]

While they insisted that ethnic identity be submerged in proletarian unity, Jews tried to keep their own ethnic identity alive—within the party. To mention one effort in this direction, *Jewish Life,* a journal of Jewish cultural affairs, was sponsored by the Jewish Bureau of the New York State Communist Party. The first anniversary of this publication was heralded in 1938 by the *Communist,* one of the official organs of the party. It would have been unheard of, as Cruse remarks, to raise official party support for a similar effort on the part of blacks—not when the section leader of the Harlem branch in the thirties was Jewish.

Racism masquerading as revolutionary purity was not an exclusive prerogative of Jewish-American communists. Between the wars and after the Second World War there were in Europe many of the type described by Stalin as "apologists for socialists." Ernest Bevin, British socialist, stressed the importance of colonies for European living standards. Communist ministers in the government of liberated France approved the French attempt to crush the nationalist struggles of the Viet-Minh and colored fellow-communist, Ho Chi Minh. These same French communists supported the repression of Algerian nationalists seeking the independence of Algeria from France. Kwame Nkrumah at the time of his ascent to power in the Gold Coast (now Ghana) was denounced as an imperialist stooge for steering the nationalist party clear of ties to British communism. "The life of independent minded Asian and African socialists like Nehru and Nkrumah," wrote George Padmore, "is certainly a difficult one! One must be either a Communist or an anti-Communist. This is typical white man's thinking, whether of the left or right . . . assertion of intellectual independence is resented by most whites and interpreted as anti-European, anti-British, anti-white. . . . Few whites can envisage a world in which they are not pushing coloured folks around. A society in which all men are equal regardless of their colour or race is to such people utopian."[24]

From Cruse's account, there was very little independent-mindedness—"pioneering achievements and creative original-ity" as he calls it—among black American communists. He means by independent-mindedness the autonomous search by blacks for the elements of the cultural compulsives that shape black American identity and life, elements deriving from the arts (music and literature especially), social life, economy, and poli-tics. In all of these areas there is a clear black signature that can be perceived by any—not just black—perceptive mind. It is, after all, whites who always said that blacks have rhythm. And there was much to perceive.

American communism was born in the same period that wit-nessed the black cultural upsurge in the twenties known as the Harlem Renaissance. The materials out of which a black Ameri-can identity could be articulated were present in music and dance (Duke Ellington, Josephine Baker), literature (Lang-ston Hughes, Claude MacKay, Zora Neale Hurston), economic thought (Booker T. Washington), social thought (W. E. B. Du-Bois), and politics (Marcus Garvey). There was much that could have engaged the attention of black communists and liberated them from white communist orthodoxies. The opportunity, however, was missed, and, for Cruse, this default represents an extreme political misfortune. The power of the black presence at the time was frittered away. A foundation on which succeeding generations of black political thinkers could build was never built.

There is a parallel situation in the wider arena of contemporary anti-mainstream social thought: the foundation for an independent black historical sense still remains to be built even though the materials for such an undertaking are abundantly present. Marxism offers a rebuttal to many of the claims of the liberal mainstream—particularly its suprahistorical enshrinement of capitalist economy and society. But it does so well within the limits of European historical experience. I have argued that in the thought of Marx himself Marxism has not articulated the specific historical counterclaims of non-Europeans. And in the hands of white Marxists it cannot speak for Asians; nor can it speak for Africans, whether in Africa, the West Indies, or in America.

Let us return to the questions with which this chapter began. Does Marxism answer the liberal misconception that Third World histories can be interpreted as a phase of European history, that the peculiar purposes and motivations that move European history are the very ones that also move Third World histories? As a corollary question, does Marxism destroy the intellectual foundations of European and white-American cultural-cum-racial chauvinisms; or does it give these, unwittingly, new ground on which to stand?

For Marx, all roads led to humanist socialism. Contrary to liberal thought, history did not end with modern capitalism. Contrary also to rationalist teleology, historical development leading to capitalism and beyond is not propelled by a "drive to rationality." It is propelled by the combined forces of economic structure, group alignments, and ultimate ends (group interests, whether earthbound or otherworldly). Assuming that each cultural formation is propelled by its own peculiar set of combined forces, it is unwarranted to think that Third World cultures were following the path of Western development. For Marxism, on these grounds, Western history is not universal history.

On the same grounds, Marx went somewhat further. He perceived that the Asiatic (African) mode was peculiar. However, he saw it this way since he assumed that capitalist industrial productivity was the necessary preamble to humanist society. He had to wonder why the Asiatic mode took so long transmuting its stagnant production relations into the modern form. On the assumption of an inevitable capitalist phase, it was indeed peculiar. On this assumption also, colonialism becomes historical necessity. And it provides the intellectual grounding for the racial and cultural chauvinisms of white Marxists. Without this assumption, Marx might have been able to see that oriental society was not peculiar. It was just different.

How should this difference be explicated? To begin with, one must take issue with Marx's characterizations of oriental society—the non-European world—as vegetative, stagnated, passive. Is it not rather that these formations enjoyed a stability that Western history has not been able to achieve? That they were in fact, as Marx said himself, "superior" because their ultimate ends were bounded by "closed shape, form and established limitation"? Is the human being in these formations "a generic being, a tribal being, a herd animal?" Is it not rather that the human enjoys a degree of material and spiritual security that is absent in the abundance of modern-day life? Where we are dealing with systems of structural inequalities, is state power simply the instrumental guarantee of ruling-class interests? Or is it weighted on the side of communal well-being?

The last question brings us to the theses of universal historical transitions in human cultural development—from migratory to settled life, and from matriarchy to patriarchy. In identifying a migratory life as the first form of existence Marx does not distinguish between hunter-gatherer nomadism and nomadic pastoralism. They must be distinguished. They do not belong to the same phase of human development. There was a universal transition only out of the first, not out of the second. Indeed the second, pastoralism, is unambiguously a postforager adaptation, but only one among others. Settled existence based on "the self-sustaining unity of manufactures and agriculture" is another. If different peoples in different cultural cradles in different geographical-ecological locations on the planet took different paths out of pristine hunter-gatherer collectivism, should their systems not be expected to manifest irreducible differences in their later cultural development? Could some formations be aggressive and others nonexpansionist? Could different traditions define the exercise of power in radically different terms?

Finally we must ask, consistent with the idea of separate development in distinct cultural cradles, was there a universal transition from matriarchy to patriarchy? Or did this "transition," in the principal theaters of its supposed occurrence (ancient societies in the Mediterranean), hide massive cultural disruption of one cradle by another—a disruption that, spanning millenia, continued down to modern times in the predatory colonial expansion of the West?

Marx begins to pry the Third World loose from the liberal interpretation of history, but as an unintended consequence of his research. The puzzles he left unsolved might point the way to an *Afro*centric understanding of historical development and human possibilities.

3

FOR THOSE WHO THINK
BLACK STUDIES CAN BE
TOO NATIONALISTIC

IN THE PRECEDING chapters I make the claim
that neither mainstream liberal sociology nor Marxism comprehends the Third World. I argue that the essential obstacle to such
comprehension is the assumption, common to both idea systems, that European cultural development is the model of cultural development in general. No doubt, many factors brought
this about. The one stressed here is the establishment of European hegemony over the globe since 1500.

Mainstream sociology, on the one hand, does not acknowledge
the role of European imperialism in creating the underdeveloped
Third World of our time. Marxism, on the other hand, does
acknowledge such a role; indeed it sees imperialism as essential,
unhappily but necessarily, to the dissolution of stagnant Third
World cultures as a prelude to their bright reconstruction in the
future. For liberalism, as well as for Marxism—despite what it
sees—European primacy is a hidden assumption. It is concealed
behind claims of scientific objectivity or historical necessity, de-
pending on whether appeal is made to the one or the other body
of thought.

However indefensible and however misleading it may be for
an adequate understanding of world history and world cultures,

the thesis of European primacy persists because of its ideological function. It has appeared in other variations and on other issues apart from those mentioned here. Two of those issues of great interest to scholars at one time, the evolution of the races and the racial (and ethnic) identity of the ancient Egyptians, are pertinent to my aims in this chapter, which are to propose a specifically Afrocentric alternative to liberal and Marxist arguments concerning Africa.

The following questions must be answered. If African society does not fit into a rationalist interpretation of history, if class struggle does not decide who gets what among traditional Africans, if African communalism and the full development of the person do not depend on abundance, what are the forces that move African history and society, and what are the cultural ideals given to map the course of the individual life? These are fundamental questions, and there are others deriving from the two issues mentioned above that are also significant.

Race determinism has become disreputable, even though, disguised in cultural ornamentation, it still has a seductive and parasitic grip on the modern intellect (see chapter one). Whatever its status today, from its beginnings in early nineteenth-century European social thought up to Franz Boas, race determinism was the paradigm that was used to explain the diversity of human behaviors. Its purpose was to put in question any suggestion that the races were equally gifted culturally, however different the expression of these gifts in different environments. Because it was the "civilized" Westerner who met the "primitive" non-Westerner, in the Western mind the test of equality was whether the "savage" races were capable of civilization—European civilization, to be precise. [1]

How this question was answered determined one's position on the evolution of races. There was, for instance, a choice between polygenism or monogenism. Did the races go through parallel and independent evolutions from multiple centers of creation (the pre-Darwinian phrasing) or multiple source populations antedating the appearance of the races (polygenism)? Or did they evolve from a common root, whether a single pair as in the Bible, or an ancestral human population that later diversified under different environmental pressures (monogenism)? And if race evolution was monogenetic, what was the race of the supposed ancestral population? Were these early humans black? Were the ancient Egyptians black?

To address questions like these involves more than a straight-forward exposition of the character of African society and history. Of course, from the perspective of cultural relativism, my perspective in this study, exposition is all that is required. However, in Western scholarship—even beyond the schools examined here—Africans and blacks everywhere appear as historical neuters and debtors to history. Hence one must properly identify them and their anthropological and historical role before describing their cultures. Without this, African cultures appear merely as exotic and, more seriously, uprooted. They appear to bear no relationship to human history or to contemporary life.

Polygenism gave intellectual grounding to racial, and consequent cultural, hierarchies in European social thought. Darwinism destroyed this grounding by positing human beginnings in a single anthropoid population; as Alfred Russell Wallace would say, species had a tendency to depart indefinitely from the original. Undoubtedly, human evolution had followed the same rule. Polygenism countered with the assumption that by the time our distinctive human capacities had evolved out of those anthropoid beginnings race formation had already occurred and raciocultural capacities had rigidified. Incidentally, both Darwin and Wallace proposed this line of response to polygenist difficulties arising in light of their work.[2] With the opening up of the fossil record from the 1850s on, the question was, what would the hominid fossil evidence show? Would it show parallel evolution—the skeletal remains of the races at the same geologic levels—or would it show their sequential appearance in the strata?

The paleontological remains known as the Grimaldi fossils are very important here.[3] These fossils were discovered in caves in the commune of Grimaldi in Italy, near the French town of

Menton. Explorations in 1873 had yielded Menton Man from the Cavillon Cave and the skeletons of two children from a cave subsequently called the Grotte des Enfants. Further explorations, resumed in this cave from 1895, unearthed four skeletons. My attention focuses on these later finds.

The four skeletons, all of which belong to modern Homo sapiens, were found at different stratigraphic levels. Two were found in the upper levels; these, along with Menton Man, have been assigned to the Cro-Magnon type, prototype of the white races. The two skeletons at the lower levels, one of an old woman and the other of a young man, were distinguished from the Cro-Magnoids that succeeded them by Professor R. Verneau, the scientist who described these finds. He assigned them to what he termed the Grimaldi Race. The Grimaldi Race was identified as black.

This identity is indicated by the characters of the skeletons. Among these may be mentioned: the disproportionate length of the leg in relation to the thigh, the forearm to the whole arm, and the lower limb to the upper limb—all proportions that "reproduce, but in greatly exaggerated degree, the characteristics presented by the modern Negro": the regular elliptical shape of the skull (seen from above) with flattened parietal bosses; broad nose depressed at the root; facial prognathism, four cusps on the upper molars and five on the lower, a dentition with "many primitive characteristics" resembling that of the Australian aborigines and seldom found among the "higher races"; "the vertical direction of the haunch bones . . . the curve of the iliac crest . . . the reduced dimensions of the great sciatic notch." All of these indicated that "the pelvis of the old woman differs from the pelvis of the modern European female, and resembles, on the contrary, that of a Negress." Of special interest is the articulation of the nose with the upper maxillary. "The floor of the nasal fossae," Boule and Vallois write, "is joined to the anterior surface of the maxillary by a groove on each side of the nasal spine, as in Negroes, instead of being bordered by a sharp edge as in the white races."[4]

The Grimaldi Negroids were found atop a layer that was Mousterian, a Middle Paleolithic culture associated with Neanderthal. Subsequently they were assigned to a higher level, the Aurignacian. Their primary antiquity is not thereby diminished. "It is none the less a fact that the Negroid skeletons date from the commencement of the Reindeer Age, a period bordering on the Mousterian, if not actually merging with it. This fact must not be lost sight of."[5] The fact was not lost sight of. Its significance was obvious; and attempts were made to deny it. Cheikh Anta Diop, a pioneer African researcher, has responded to these attempts.

The proposers of one stratagem, unable to dismiss the reality of the paleontological evidence of a primary black humanity, argued for keeping the question of an equally ancient white humanity open—it was simply that the evidence for this had not yet been found. " 'At that period [40,000+ years ago]' offered one scholar, 'the three races must necessarily have already existed on earth with their own well-defined characteristics; archeology will one day find specimens of white men as old as the first Negro Aurignacians. When the latter lived in Europe, the white race must have been elsewhere, in some location not yet excavated. But its existence at that period cannot be doubted.' "[6] Such intellectual caution is too precious. Had the evidence pointed to a primary white humanity cautiousness would never have been proposed. Nevertheless, it is science, indeed white scientific research, ironically enough, that compels us to conclude that the first humans were black.

Others oppose this conclusion by disputing the factualness of the skeletal characters that define the Grimaldi Race as black. One scholar has denied the prognathism of the skulls by trying to explain it away. In his explanation, prognathism resulted from the loss of lower molars in the case of the old woman, and dislocation of the teeth and damage to the skull over time in the case of the young man. However, as Diop points out, alveolar prognathism of the teeth is distinct from facial prognathism of the jawbones, "which is unquestionably the case in the adoles-

cent as in the old woman." It is significant that the attempt to re-
interpret properties of the skeletons makes no reference to the resemblance of the pelvis of the old woman to "that of a Negress,"
nor to the junction of the nasal fossae with the upper maxillary—
"an observation which suffices to ruin his whole theory."[7]

The Grimaldi Race and related types were widely dispersed.
The evidence of dispersal is paleontological and archaeological.
Fossil remains of this race have been discovered at neolithic levels
in Asia (Indonesia, Southern India, Mesopotamia, Syria) and Eu-
rope (the British Isles, France, Spain); and at paleolithic levels in
Africa.

At a time when European researchers, except for Darwin,
could not conceive of an African beginning for humanity, it was
proposed that the Grimaldi Race arose in Asia. Since then Africa
has yielded from the Sahara the Asselar skeleton, which closely
resembles the Grimaldi skeletons; Olduvai Man; the very ancient
(lower paleolithic) Saldanha Man, considered along with Rhode-
sian Man to be proto-Australian; and the Boskop and Florisbad
skeletons, regarded as ancestral to the Bushmen and Hottentot
races. Cro-Magnon Man does not appear in Africa south of the
Sahara. He emerges, at the end of the upper Paleolithic, only in
North Africa, and then as a Cro-Magnoid with Ethiopian features—depressed root of the nose, wide (platyrrhinian) nasal
aperture. He is regarded by Boule and Vallois as being more
primitive in degree of physical evolution than Cro-Magnon of
Europe. They assumed that both types derived from a common
origin in Asia and developed parallel to one another, European
Cro-Magnon evolving further. Today, in light of the wealth of
fossils unearthed in Africa, we may assume that Mechta Man
simply crossed the Mediterranean after his late subspeciation
from the black races on the northern borders of the homeland of
humanity.

Aurignacian art also attests to the ancient black presence. This
art is the earliest that humanity created. Paleolithic cave paintings in Europe are a precious part of our cultural treasury, but

they were not executed by Europeans. Consider this comment on paleolithic cave paintings in Southern Africa:

> The resemblance of all these works of art to those of the Upper Paleolithic in French and Spanish caves has often been noted: there are the same preferences in the choice of subject, animals being the most common, the same realism, the same fidelity of attitude, the same skill in reproduction, the same technique, and even the same weakness in drawing the human figure. All this had been invoked in support of the theory that the Bushmen were the ancestors of our Aurignacians and Magdalenians. Certain similarities between the industries of the two groups have been advanced in corroboration of this idea.

"Bushmen Art," another comment states, "is extraordinarily like that of our caves. . . . The centres are united by a long, connected series of works of art, from France to the Cape by way of Spain, North Africa, the Sudan, the Chad, and the Transvaal. This almost uninterrupted series leads us to regard the African continent as a centre of important migrations, which at certain times may have played a great part in the stocking of Southern Europe. Finally, we must not forget that the Grimaldi Negroid skeletons show many points of resemblance with Bushmen skeletons."[8]

These Bushmen types left us images of their women, those steatopygous (with protruding buttocks) Aurignacian statuettes found widely scattered all over Europe as far away as Eastern Russia (Kostienski and Gagarino). Famous among these sculptures are the Venus of Willendorf, the Venus of Lespugue, and the Venus of Brassempouy (La Poire). The statuettes share a set of affinities with Bushmen women: hairstyles suggesting narrow plaits (parallel lines on the head) or corn rows (crisscrossing lines), well-known black coiffures; large cylindrical, pendulous breasts; prominent belly with fatty tissue overhanging the pubes; greatly developed hips, often steatopygous; fleshy thighs; developed nymphae suggesting the apron of Bushman women. Plate 221 in *Fossil Men* reproduces a collection of figurines recovered from the Grimaldi caves. The two figurines juxtaposed at the bottom right of the plate show a steatopygous statue and a photograph of a Bushman woman in profile. The profiles approach identity, particularly in the area of the backward swerve of the buttocks.

There is similarity in ethnographic practices as well. Necklaces accompany the bodies of women and children in Bushman burials. One of these necklaces is exactly like those found at Menton.

As with fossil evidence, paleolithic art has been questioned as testimony to an ancestral black humanity. One scholar, as reported by Diop, thinks that in interpreting the steatopygic statuettes, "it is necessary to accept the idea of a fertility cult." And why is this? " 'For,' he states, 'it would be incredible that France, Italy, and Siberia could have been inhabited by people of the same Negroid race, all of whose women were steatopygic.' "[9] Other interpretations have been suggested that are preoccupied with the same concerns, even though this is not explicitly acknowledged. Here is one: paleolithic men liked their women fat. (A remarkable coincidence: their fantasies looked like Bushwomen.) Or again: fatty bodies were adaptive in the arctic environment of the time.[10] (But why were the male figures so lithe?)

These arguments, as well as those against the Negroness of the Grimaldi fossils, are not just the clever sophistries of individual scientists. They are institutionalized in mainstream scholarship. *Fossil Men* was first published in 1921 and republished in 1957. Diop's *The African Origin of Civilization* first appeared in 1955 and was published again in 1967. Yet the arguments against black origins make their way unchanged from William Howells, *Mankind in the Making* (1959), through John Geipel, *The Europeans* (1969), to Joseph Birdsell, *Human Evolution* (1972, 1975).

Birdsell's book, let it be noted, is a modern introductory text for students to what he terms the "new" physical anthropology, the emphasis on process according to neo-Darwinian principles being the new element. In that sense it is different from the Howells book. Commendably, and as one would expect today, its materials on race classification and evolution may be read as a statement on the biological equality of the races, a complex statement that cannot be presented here. Yet Birdsell assigns the Grimaldi Negroids to the Cro-Magnon race on the basis of arguments designed to make black people and black history disappear into white shadows, arguments he could answer since the answers are already available. The book's defense of racial equality is therefore empty, a purely formalistic exercise. It carefully ignores reference to the cultural anteriority of blacks, an important matter in our time, when blacks are regarded as biologically equal but culturally deprived.

Birdsell, and for that matter Howells, has read Boule and Vallois. But he has read their work selectively. Often enough, the French scientists are guarded in their conclusions. But they do not avoid the evidence by clever interpretations. More than once they note the significance of what paleontological and archeological evidence suggests: black anteriority anthropologically and, most interestingly, in the peopling of Europe. They quote Verneau: "We must therefore admit that an almost Negro element lived in South-Western Europe towards the Mid Quaternary Era, between the Spy race and the Cro-Magnon race."[11] This is the "incredible" fact that Birdsell must lose sight of. For this reason, despite the wealth of new data he offers on human evolution, especially from biology, he impoverishes the anthropological and cultural synthesis offered by his predecessors.

No doubt, to accept the Aurignacian industries and art in Europe as the creations of black peoples is a political blow to the Eurocentric theory of black benightedness awaiting white enlightenment. Yet it is a scientifically established fact, as neutral as the fact that the sun rises in the east. The impoverishment of our understanding of anthropology and history lies in not treating it as such. And it has not been so treated because white history has had to insist for a long time that blacks had no history of consequence. Who are the blacks? They are the first humans in history. No less, but no more either. To put it in different terms, black anteriority anthropologically and culturally is an argument against white supremacy; but it is not an argument for black supremacy. The thesis simply states that blacks, contrary to white claims, have made signal contributions to human cultural experience. And it notes that they were the first to do so.

Black anteriority is not confined only to the era of primitive (pristine) human development. It stands at the head of the leap into civilization, civilization in the Nile Valley among a black African people, a people known as the Egyptians. On the whole, Egyptology does not accept that the ancient Egyptians were a black people.

> Ancient Egypt was stolen from Africa by nineteenth-century Egyptologists whose doctrine was nourished by the African slave trade, the sugar empire, and the cotton kingdom. Many scientists during this period were loathe to associate black folks with the human race, much less with civilization. Hence it was early determined that not only black people be excluded from Egypt, but that Egypt itself, through ingenious anthropological manipulation, be excluded from Africa. . . . Never before or since has such a mockery been made of human history in the name of racial superiority and under the auspices of anthropological pursuit. Science bowed before race prejudice and truth recoiled in panic. [12]

The exclusion of Egypt from Africa is accomplished by many stratagems. Consider, for instance, the division of Africa into Southern Africa (below the Sahara) and Northern Africa. The division suggests that Northern Africa is not African—it is European, or it belongs to the East. Why did James Breasted create an Institute of Oriental Studies at Chicago and place Egyptology as an academic discipline within that institute? Imagine Egyptology as a discipline within an institute of African studies, and what is at issue becomes clear.

Scholars choose to forget that desiccation in the Sahara is a recent environmental event (2000 B.C.). The region in ancient times witnessed the flow of human migrations and ideas throughout the continent. It never limited access to the Nile Valley in the formative years of Egyptian civilization. [13]

Rock paintings in the Tassili mountains suggest that in the

last wet period the Sahara was a grassland that supported herding animals and an area of independent plant domestication. Animal herds (and herders) are a frequent subject of the paintings. Was the Sahara the original home of their domestication? Fossil bones of tamable cattle found there support this possibility. It is known that domesticated cattle roamed the Sahara in 5500 B.C. In the paintings cattle often appear with horns twisted according to the fancy of the human masters of these animals. They anticipate cattle with similarly twisted horns that appear in Egyptian frescoes. Did the animal-headed gods and goddesses of Egypt travel from the Tassili rock paintings of human figures dressed in animal heads and tails, migrating with populations that sought to escape the increasing dessication of the land? Did pharaonic costume derive from hunters of the once-watered Sahara?

The mummified body of a black infant has been discovered in the Fezzan. It has been assigned a date of 3500 B.C., older than the oldest Egyptian mummy. This evidence and that of the Tassili frescoes are part of a larger body of data that roots the cultural evolution of Egypt in African beginnings.

Apart from the traits mentioned, Egypt shares with other African societies totemism, circumcision, divine kingship, caste organization of the social structure (without caste avoidance), and matrilineality (matriarchy, by which is meant not female dominance but sexual equality). Taken in combination, they distinguish African from Indo-European cultures. [14]

Some Egyptologists would grant that Egyptian culture was African. But then they proceed to transform Egyptians into white people by intellectual sleight of hand or by sheer non sequiturs. Breasted tells us that "the conclusion once maintained by some historians, that the Egyptian was of African Negro origin, is now refuted." He also tells us that the forefathers of the Egyptians were related to East African peoples such as the Galla, Somali, and Bega; and he finds that "the representations of the early Puntites, or Somali people, on the Egyptian monuments, show striking resemblances to the Egyptians themselves." [15] Thus the thesis that Egyptians were black is refuted by comparing them to the Galla, Bega, and Somali. This makes sense only to minds committed to a desperate agility of the intellect.

E. Wallis Budge, one of those agile minds, affirms that neolithic peoples in Egypt were African and thinks it reasonable to assume that they were related to all of the other Nile Valley inhabitants. But he thinks that the pyramid builders in Egypt were a different people who came either from Asia or the Northern Mediterranean. "It is quite certain," he says, "that many of their physical characteristics were 'European.'" [16] Now it is certain that Budge saw the bust of King Zoser, the Third Dynasty pharaoh credited with inaugurating colossal architecture in stone; it was he who built the step pyramid tomb at Saqqara. In profile (plate 6 in *The African Origin of Civilization*), the bust shows a face with fleshy nose, thick lips, and prognathism. How can features such as these be made European? One scholar managed to do it.

Champollion-Figeac, brother of Champollion the Younger, the man who (in a parallel development with the Englishman, Thomas Young) deciphered Egyptian hieroglyphic, comments on a remark made by Constantin de Volney that the Copts, who have a bloated face, puffed-up eyes, flat nose, and thick lips are descended from the Egyptians. Volney also noted that they resemble the Sphinx, the face of which is clearly black; and he recalled Herodotus' eyewitness description of the Egyptians as a people with black skin and woolly hair. Figeac adroitly rescues a white identity from this testimony: "These two physical qualities [black skin and wooly hair]," he writes, "do not suffice to characterize the Negro race." With this kind of physical anthropological logic it is not surprising that he finds "Volney's conclusion as to the Negro origin of the ancient Egyptian civilization forced and inadmissible." [17] Indeed.

The white man with black skin was a fleshless anthropological fantasy. But he became a pseudoexistent being by the power of a word, *Hamite*. [18] The term had a flexible usefulness. It could define blacks as an accursed people, a race with a curse of servitude it had inherited from its biblical ancestor, Ham, the youngest son of Noah, who had been cursed by his father. The curse fell most heavily on Canaan, one of Ham's sons, and his children. It neatly justified the Hebrew subjugation of the Canaanites who were in the land when Father Abraham and his people arrived. It was expanded in the Babylonian Talmud in the sixth century A.D. and in rabbinical commentaries on the Genesis story in the Middle Ages. In our time it served to legitimize the enslavement and oppression of African peoples.

The Napoleonic conquest of Egypt in 1798 opened up that land to intensive archaeological study. It was during this time that Champollion the Younger deciphered the hieroglyphic. French scholars, including Champollion, concluded that the ancient Egyptians were negroids, a conclusion reached years earlier by Count Volney. It was to this " 'race of negroes,' Volney reflected, 'at present our slaves, and objects of our contempt, we owe our arts, sciences.' "[19] The problem was how to make the curse on Ham and the God-ordained servitude of blacks square with the discovery that blacks originated the oldest civilization, the civilization from which Europe derived much of its cultural inspiration—its religion, art, philosophy, and science. The answer was found in a new anthropological meaning given to the term Hamite.

Revising the biblical account scholars decided that only Canaan had been cursed. Ham's other sons, Mizraim (Egypt) and Kush (Ethiopia), had not been cursed, and in fact had prospered. Egyptians became one of the Hamitic groups assigned to the white races, a white people with brown, red, reddish-brown, or dark red skin—but remarkably never with white skin. Scholars could now maintain with a straight face that blacks had never been capable of civilization.

The Egyptians themselves say that they came from the south (the upper Nile), ancient Ethiopia. Diodorus of Sicily recounts the claim of the Ethiopians that Egypt was a colony of Ethiopia and that Egyptians derive their laws and cultural practices from that more ancient civilization, these practices including sculpture, writing, and the honor of kings as gods. Strabo thinks it

was the Egyptians who settled Ethiopia. Such remarks among
the ancient writers would make no sense if it were not obvious to
them that Egyptians and Ethiopians belonged to the same race.
Despite the weight of evidence many Egyptologists have insis-
tently sought a European or Asian origin for the Egyptian people
and civilization. [20]

A European origin for Egyptians has no factual basis. It is
enough to point out that not one of the pristine civilizations—in
the Nile Valley, Mesopotamia, India, China, Middle America,
and the Andes—developed in Europe. As for an Asian origin,
investigations do not reveal whites in a presumed civilizing
role. What they unveil is other worlds, contemporary with
Egypt, where blacks are again in the historical vanguard. These
blacks, like African blacks, were called Ethiopians by the ancient
Greeks, because they were, consistent with the etymological
roots for the word in the Greek language, burnt faces.

The term *Ethiopia* was used by ancient Greek and Latin au-
thors to include the Sudan, Egypt, Arabia, Palestine, Western
Asia, and India—a territory considerably larger than modern
Ethiopia today. [21] It was the black inhabitants of these lands who
were the agents of the Neolithic Revolution, the foundation of
civilized life, in the Fertile Crescent (Western Asia and the Nile
Valley) and India.

A human type known as the Natufian, which dates from the
late Mesolithic (about 10,000 years ago), is credited with beginning a primitive agriculture in Palestine (Canaan, later Phoe-
nicia, as it was known in ancient times). [22] It is related to similar
types found in the Near East, North Africa, Malta, predynastic
Egypt and Mugem (Portugal). The Natufian is the prevailing
type in later neolithic populations in Jericho and Megiddo as
well as in Mesopotamia.

Natufians were short, men averaging five feet three inches,
women five feet; and dolichocephalic (long-headed). Keith and
Vallois, the scientists who described them, "noted a certain degree of facial projection and a low-vaulted nose suggestive of

negroid affinities." Hence, even though they are considered "a primitive or emergent Mediterranean type,"[23] the negroid affinities should leave no confusion as to their racial identity: they are nothing other than a black population. Indeed, Harry Shapiro draws attention to their resemblance to paleolithic skulls found in Europe, a reference to the Grimaldi Race that has already been described.

The black presence at the birth of civilization in Mesopotamia and India is also a well-attested fact.[24] The earliest phase of Mesopotamian civilization is the Sumerian phase. John G. Jackson tells us that in Assyrio-Babylonian inscriptions Sumerians are designated as the blackheads or black-faced people. One scholar thinks they were an Elamite colony. Researchers discovered in an Elamite tomb "a panel which depicted a person of rank. . . . The most curious thing about this person, of whom I found the lower part of the face, the beard, the neck and hand, was that he was black . . . the wrist is covered with bracelets and fingers grasp the long staff which became under the Archimenides the emblem of sovereign power. . . . The hands and the feet were black. . . . Now, the owner of the staff, the master of the citadel, is black; it is thus very possible that Elam was the prerogative of a Black dynasty and if one refers to the characteristics of the figure already found, of an Ethiopian dynasty."

Sir Henry Rawlinson suggests the reasonableness of the Ethiopian and Egyptian origin of Sumerian people and culture. He draws attention to the similarity of Sumerian and Egyptian writing and alphabets; the biblical genealogies, which say that Kush (Ethiopia) and Mizraim (Egypt) were brothers and that from the former sprang Nimrod (Babylonia); the vocabulary of the early Babylonians, which is Kushite; and the traditions of Babylonia, which indicate a connection in ancient times between Ethiopia, Southern Arabia, and the cities of the Lower Euphrates.[25]

As for India, the early inhabitants there were "a dark-skinned, broad-nosed people whom, without knowing the origin of the word, we call Dravidians."[26] It was they who built the ancient cities, Mohenjo Daro, Chanhu Daro, and Harappa. The Vedic hymns written by the Aryan invaders about 1000 B.C. describe these inhabitants as black-skinned barbarians, Dasas, or slaves.

What has been said should indicate that no appeal can be made to Asia to find a white origin for Egyptian civilization since in Asia, as in Ethiopia (Nubia) and Egypt, it was blacks who were the civilizing force.

Although the indebtedness of Europe to black cultural ante-riority, most especially to Egyptian civilization, has already been mentioned, it bears repeating. Commenting on Diop's presenta-tion of this idea, Immanuel Wallerstein wrote: "This bold hy-pothesis, which is not presented without supporting data, has the interesting effect of inverting Western cultural assumptions. For, Diop argues, if the ancient Egyptians were Negroes, then European civilization is but a derivation of African achieve-ment." Diop's own remarks on this point are worth quoting at some length:

> According to the unanimous testimony of the Ancients, first the Ethiopians and then the Egyptians created and raised to an extraor-dinary stage of development all the elements of civilization, while other peoples especially the Eurasians, were still deep in barbarism. The explanation for this must be sought in the material conditions in which the accident of geography had placed them at the be-ginning of time. For man to adapt, these conditions required the invention of sciences complemented by the creation of arts and religion.
>
> It is impossible to stress all that the world, particularly the Hel-lenistic world, owed to the Egyptians. The Greeks merely con-tinued and developed, sometimes partially, what the Egyptians had invented. By virtue of their materialistic tendencies, the Greeks stripped those inventions of the religious idealistic shell in which the Egyptians had enveloped them. On the one hand, the rugged life on the Eurasian plains apparently intensified the materialistic instinct of the peoples living there; on the other hand it forged moral values diametrically opposed to Egyptian moral values which stemmed from a collective, sedentary, relatively easy, peaceful life, once it had been regulated by a few social laws.

To the extent that the Egyptians were horrified by theft, nomadism, and war, to the same extent these practices were highly moral on the Eurasian plains. Only a warrior killed on the battlefield could enter Valhalla, the Germanic paradise. Among the Egyptians, no felicity was possible except for the deceased who could prove at the Tribunal of Osiris, that he had been charitable to the poor and had never sinned. This was the antithesis of the spirit of rapine and conquest that generally characterized the peoples of the north, driven, in a sense, away from a country unfavored by Nature. In contrast, existence was so easy in the valley of the Nile, a veritable Garden of Eden, between two deserts, that the Egyptians tended to believe that Nature's benefits poured down from the sky. They finally adored it in the form of an Omnipotent Being. Their early materialism—in other words their vitalism—would henceforth become a materialism transposed to the sky, a metaphysical materialism, if one may call it that.

On the contrary, the horizons of the Greeks were never to pass beyond material, visible man, the conqueror of hostile Nature. On the earth, everything gravitated around him; the supreme objective of art was to reproduce his exact likeness. In the "heavens," paradoxically, he alone was to be found. . . . Thus, when the Greek borrowed the Egyptian god, a real god in the full sense of the word, provided with all the moral perfections that stem from sedentary life, he could understand that deity only by reducing him to the level of man. Consequently, the adoptive Pantheon of the Greek was merely another humanity. This anthropomorphism, in this particular case, was characteristic of the Greek mind. Strictly speaking, the Greed miracle does not exist, for if we try to analyze the process of adapting Egyptian values to Greece, there is obviously nothing miraculous about it in the intellectual sense of the term.[27]

What Diop says in this passage should serve to remind us that Greek (and European) indebtedness was not simply the result of a borrowing. African inventions—later, Africans themselves—were appropriated, often enough as a result of force and destruction as with Alexander, the Ptolemies, the Caesars, and the modern imperialists in our own time. Appropriation is indeed the appropriate term even where one is referring to dissemination of Egyptian knowledge through the schooling of Greeks—Anaximander, Thales, Democritus, Pythagoras, Plato, Aristotle, for instance—in Egypt, because moderns do not acknowledge the Egyptian origin of Greek science and philosophy.[28] Furthermore, as Diop states, it is essential to understand that the cultural milieu of the early Europeans made them put what they had acquired to uses quite different from the original Egyptian purposes. Recognizing this makes it easier for us to grasp why Europeans never adopted Egyptian, or more generally African, values, particularly those values that gave direction to individual life and organized the social structure.

Consideration of these values brings us back to the questions posed at the beginning of the chapter. If African systems were never moving in accordance with the Western rationalist telos, what ends shaped African cultural development? Are group interests decided through class struggle? And if not, what decides them? If abundance is not at the basis of African communalism and personal development, what did African sensibilities depend on instead? These questions are meant to suggest that African systems are different from Western systems. It is African values, I suggest, that make the difference.

The theory of rationalist evolution sets itself the task of explaining the origins of industrial abundance in the West, why such a goal was ever espoused and what social forces brought it into being. The class struggle—and interest-group politics, its mainstream derivation—explains the distribution of this abundance. In African systems a different reality presents itself for explanation, a different explanation—that reality is the extraordinary historical persistence of the African form of society.

Consider Western experience. The rationalist development of the West is an evolution driven by social struggles. The West has witnessed the revolutionary destruction and reordering of economy, class structure, political form. And this development set a kind of pure individualism free from the uncertain grip of communal traditions, insofar as these existed in the West. This has had profound consequences for the moral order.

Basil Davidson makes the following observation:

> Britain lives today, we are told by sociologists, amidst a "jumble of ethical precepts, now bereft of their significance . . . within a wasteland littered with the debris of broken convictions." For a world where the ideal is one of personal accumulation, the good of the individual is set in opposition to the good of the community . . . and the good of the community goes increasingly to the wall. No matter what lip service to the general weal may continue to be paid in Sunday observances or other ritual proclamations, we become communities without any visible means of moral support.[29]

The well-being of groups and individuals is not prescribed by morality. It is determined by the play of power struggles. Retention of power, however, is uncertain. Certainly the poor have seldom had it; and they have never held it for long. As is well known, idea systems, whether theories of stratification or metaphysical or biological determinisms that justify (some would say explain) poverty in the midst of industrial abundance, have also served in defense of colonial theft and rapine. In an age of a sophisticated social science this should pose itself as a conundrum. But social science, and not just social science, long ago parted company with ethical judgment, in an unhappy declension from the great Max Weber. A different outcome could hardly have been expected.

African worlds present a striking contrast. I have already discussed the antiquity of black civilizations. Their longevity spans the millennia since Nubian beginnings. "Blacks slowly penetrated into the heart of the continent, spreading out in all directions and dislodging the Pygmies. They founded states which developed and maintained relations with the mother valley until it was stifled by the foreigner. From south to north, these were Nubia and Egypt; from north to south, Nubia and Zimbabwe; from east to west, Nubia, Ghana [a state said to be in existence at the time of the Pharaohs], Ife; from east to southwest Nubia, Chad, the Congo; from west to east, Nubia and Ethiopia."[30] Not one of these states collapsed from internal social crises even though they were systems with clearly defined inequalities.

Inequality and social peace together? Does the one not exclude the other? The answer to the puzzle lies in the fate of ordinary African men and women in their societies. Louis B. Leakey, criticizing European assumptions of superiority, which rested on pride in Western technological accomplishments, offered the opinion that in certain ways Africans were superior to their invaders. He noted that long before European incursion Bantu peoples had an effective system of family planning. They imposed the death penalty only on persistent murderers, under the assumption that a person who had committed murder must have suffered extreme provocation and was unlikely to do it again; such a person and his family were required to make restitution to the bereaved family. He observed that African women had far greater freedom and greater rights than their Western counterparts to live their own lives, and they enjoyed considerable sexual freedom. "Let me remind you," Leakey told his audience, "that before the coming of the white man, social organization in many African tribes was such that tragedies such as destitute widows and orphans, unloved lonely spinsters, unmarried mothers, and aged and uncared for elderly people were unheard of and indeed could not occur, while prostitution was unknown."[31]

More than six hundred years before Leakey made his observations, Ibn Battuta recorded similar impressions of the Empire of Mali. He found admirable the small number of acts of injustice that the blacks, more than other peoples, abhorred and that the sultan consequently never pardoned; the complete safety one enjoyed in the land because there was no reason to fear brigands, thieves, or ravishers; the safekeeping of the goods of white people, which blacks never confiscated even when they were of great value, but left entrusted to a white person until they could be claimed by their rightful owners.[32]

Commentaries from antiquity paint the same picture of black

life. Homer himself spoke of the blameless Ethiopians. It was among them, he remarked, that the gods took their yearly sojourn to feast for twelve days.[33]

African life was not always peaceful. There was warfare. But it was a traditional kind of warfare, never aimed at biological extermination. Basil Davidson describes the traditional practice of war among the Ngoni, one of the peoples who, under the leadership of that formidable military genius, Shaka, would become grim and blood-stained agents in the creation of the Zulu empire. Hostilities were assigned to a particular day. On that day warrior youths accompanied by cheering women and girls marched out in a blaze of excitement. The chosen champions of each party would face off in single combat. The wounded would be taken by the visitors to be ransomed with cattle before the day's end. Mutual condolences would be exchanged over the slain.[34]

The main object of such warfare, we are told, was to overcome or scare the adversary, not to kill, if that could be avoided. Fearsome masks and blood-curdling screams were an integral part of military tactics. Sometimes hostile encounters were punctuated by rest periods. Combatants would meet at streams to refresh themselves and laugh at each others' jokes until they were summoned back to battle. Victors often provided escape routes for the vanquished and would pretend to be unaware of them.[35]

Not only did Africans traditionally attempt to inhibit the destructiveness of war, some of them created institutional arrangements to avoid it altogether. Reference was made in an earlier chapter to the Kung. They avoid war because it is dangerous: someone might get killed. They depend instead on those who are skilled in defusing quarrels. The Tallensi think similarly. Their moral order frowns on quarrels, and fights seldom occur. For them, the ideal relationship between neighbors is one of peace. Their chiefs and Earth-priests represent two sets of principal forces that sustain their society. These forces must be kept in equilibrium. Tradition reveals to these functionaries, and to the people, what must be done.[36]

Most interesting are the Lovedu. They live within a state system headed by a "king" who is a woman—always. Their traditions stress "willingness to compromise, moderation, having neither more nor less than anybody else." They disapprove of boastfulness and do not praise courage. The choice of a woman as leader was an institutional stratagem designed to eliminate conflict among heirs to succession; and, strange as it may seem, to make them safe among their more warlike neighbors. Who would attack a queen who commanded spiritual armies, as the Lovedu queen was known to do? It is said that even Shaka did not disturb their peace. "There were no policemen or warriors in Loveduland and had not been since women had begun to rule."[37]

What supported such practices? Chancellor Williams suggests that "the highly humane aspect of African warfare that puzzled many Western visitors doubtlessly developed from the widespread recognition of lineage or kinship ties. . . . It is quite clear that in early Africa 'war' was not much more than a frightful game when among themselves. . . . Lineage, then, was the most powerful and effective force for unity and stability in early Africa."[38]

The point is well taken. Kinship, however, regulated more than the conduct of war. It also regulated the conduct of daily life: economic activity, politics, social relations, and moral values—ancestral beliefs couched in religious and philosophical terms. Kinship controlled the most simple and the most complex social formations; it was the basis of society through all the stages of cultural evolution—band, tribe, chiefdom, and state. Contrary to an accepted tradition in anthropological thought, in Africa, upon emergence of the state, territory did not replace kinship as the basis of the social system.

The pervasive role of kinship in primitive band societies is well established. Bands (Kung, Pygmy) are not structurally differentiated. The kinship unit suffices for all the necessary societal functions: reproduction, subsistence, political control, recreational and artistic activities, ritual activities, socialization into the traditional complex of practical activities and moral values (rules of etiquette and ethics). These are societies without governments (central authorities that command an administration). Social order therefore depends on adherence to rules of ethical conduct hallowed by tradition. For instance, the cardinal rules of economic life are cooperation and sharing (reciprocity). It is not simply that these are sensible and practical answers to the problem of survival. They are also morally binding. Doubtless, the intimacies of a kinship that embraced all members of the community gave these rules their force.

Bands are usually contrasted with states. One expects to find in a state that the social egalitarianism and the pervasive kin structure of the band have disappeared. Nevertheless social inequality first makes its appearance in societies still organized on a kinship basis.[39] With the invention of agriculture and animal husbandry kin structure undergoes a novel reorganization. The corporate kin group emerges, encountered in Africa as the corporate descent group—often enough as a matrilineage. Some corporate kin groups permit the development of economic forces and harbor increasing inequalities and progressively more rigid social differentiation. Ultimately, perhaps as a result of continuing immigration of strangers, the kinship basis of society disappears, and we enter the era of history dominated by classes and their social struggles.

Basil Davidson finds that the common contrast drawn between societies without governments and societies with governments does not accurately describe African systems. Even in large states with kings, executive offices, standing armies, and hierarchies of wealth, "the old authority of kinship remained of critical influence in deciding what was politically done or not done . . . men acquired office by virtue of their positions in the kinship structure, and exercised power by sanctions whose ultimate creation depended not on any royal will, but on ancestral mandate." As Davidson sees it, "there is no point along the kinship continuum at which a true dividing line may be drawn between centrally ruled societies on the one hand, and 'governmentless' or 'stateless' societies on the other hand."[40]

African kinship systems may be regarded as cultural inventions of primal significance. It was the kinship unit that invented and generationally transmitted successful strategies of adaptation, social relations that optimized peaceful living, and the ethical rules that made observance of these ways compulsory. These ethical systems stressed not individual rights but individual obligations, because it was the material and moral health of the community that guaranteed the survival of the individual. "The moral order was robustly collective."[41]

Kinship and its attendant values undergirded all societies of traditional Africa. Kinship structure changed to accommodate the principle of descent. Economic life, class systems, and political structures also changed. But collective well-being remained a moral constant from band through tribe and chiefdom to state. If Africans everywhere adopted the kinship complex it was because they understood its social efficacy. Its endurance is explained by what it did. As Basil Davidson said, it resolved conflict, facilitated cooperation, promoted social unity, and, let us not forget, created societies without orphans, widows, and lonely old people. In short, it delivered the things that Africans valued. That is why the kinship complex survived the transition from the band to the state. But exactly how did it work in state systems?

How do we explain the durability of these state systems despite the structured social inequalities within them? Much emphasis has been placed here on communal values and ethical imperatives that directed the conduct of life as a principal force in system maintenance. The question is, why did these structured divisions not finally imprison observance of the rules of everyday life in a morass of insoluble social contradictions? So insoluble in fact that one would expect systemic collapse and alteration.

The answer lies in the nature of traditional social divisions; they were more functional than they were hierarchical and antagonistic. Many Africanists have observed that class stratification was generally not rigid in Africa.

Most African societies belong to an economic order very different from ours. Theirs is mainly a subsistence economy with a rudimentary differentiation of productive labor and with no machinery for the accumulation of wealth in the form of commercial or industrial capital. If wealth is accumulated it takes the form of consumption goods and amenities or is used for the support of additional dependents. Hence it tends to be rapidly dissipated again and does not give rise to permanent class divisions. Distinctions of rank, status, or occupation operate independently of differences of wealth.[42]

If not wealth, what were the perquisites of rank? They were mainly ritual and honorific entitlements, although they were sometimes accompanied by material rewards and privileges. In any case, the effect of distinctions in material living conditions was not to create and maintain communities of desperately impoverished people. As is the practice in economies based on redistribution, it was the function of the central authority and its village and town representatives—the agencies that accumulated wealth—to aid communities in distress. There was no unequal struggle to exist as a driving structural tension in African society.

What determined the right to rank was lineage seniority, as judged by proximity of descent from founding ancestors, both female and male. But that entitlement could only be validated by strict observance of the communal duties and responsibilities imposed on rank and power by ancestral tradition. The effect of such control was to put a decisive limit on the use of power as a personal or group prerogative.

A significant aspect of this limit was that it clearly defined power transgressions. Just as clearly defined was the aim of all those countervailing pressures that had the constitutional function of preventing or sanctioning such transgressions. As M. Fortes and E. E. Evans-Pritchard phrased it, there was only one theory of government. In principle, constitutional checks on power were set in motion to restore power to its traditional boundaries. It was never a question of the forcible transmutation of the form in which power was exercised.[43]

All of this was consistent with the real meaning of divine kingship. Despite the reverence attached to their persons, divine kings were not autocrats. Administrators represented them in local governments. But these same administrators represented the local community and its interests against the king. Kings were honored as divinities because they were the living embodiment of ancestral powers at one time ritually invested in many lineage heads. In the divine king, it is said, a people's unity survived.[44]

What exploded this form and destroyed this unity was nothing internal. Instead, it was the intrusion into Africa and the ancient black world of white and Semitic peoples who brought a radically different temper and a value system hostile to the practice of life they encountered in Africa.

The latest episode of white intrusion into African society is modern-era European colonialism. I have already made the point that liberal sociology, assuming rationalist evolution to be a universal cultural tendency, interprets colonialism as a force somehow historically chosen to propel Africa toward the universally fated end of rationalist development. In this interpretation, the West was not so much a dominant colonial presence as it was an exemplary beacon to other cultures marching at a slower pace toward rationalist fulfillment. As for earlier intrusions, the liberal tradition does not recognize them.

The Marxist interpretation is closer to the truth. It understands the Western presence to be rapacious and destructive, but it sees colonialism as a necessary stimulus to move stagnant cultures to a level of material production that could support modern socialism, the only social form it is felt that could deliver humanity from the evils of exploitation and class struggle. Of course, because they are hierarchical, stagnant systems untouched by colonialism also need modern socialist deliverance. Even without the colonial impulse, they too would make the explosive passage to socialism, although perhaps over a longer course. This must follow since, like other systems, they had experienced the universal historical transitions adopted in the Marxist tradition: from primitive communism to the eras of inequality and exploitation, and from matriarchy to patriarchy.

One might say that Engels intended that the transition from matriarchy to patriarchy be read as the inside story of how the transition from primitive communism occurred. The truth is, it was not a transition at all—certainly not a universal one. By interpreting as evidence of this transition the data on the ancient world available to him, Engels failed to perceive what the data actually implied: the earliest European incursion into the black world, an incursion as destructive as the modern colonial episode. Without this interpretation, the tradition he helped establish might have seen something other than stagnation in the Asiatic—or African—mode of production, something more instructive for the socialist imagination.

Before developing this point, I should say something concerning the thesis that the shift from matriarchy to patriarchy that Engels observed in ancient times was not an evolutionary transition; rather, the argument I present here goes, it recorded cultural disruption in the ancient Mediterranean world by the ancestors of the Europeans. My authority here is Cheikh Anta Diop.

In *The Cultural Unity of Black Africa,* Diop criticizes the classical theory of matriarchy as a universal stage in human history. The first step in his argument is a comment on the version of the theory offered by Bachofen, an important source for Engels:

> A first important criticism which can be made of the theory of Bachofen is that it makes an important omission, which has not been given sufficient prominence. The demonstration of a universal transition from matriarchy to patriarchy is only scientifically acceptable if it can be proved that this internal evolution has definitely taken place among a specific people. Now this condition has never been fulfilled in the works of the author. It has never been possible to determine the existence of a historical period during which the Greeks and the Romans might have lived under matriarchy. This

difficulty is gotten round by replacing the Greeks and Romans by aboriginal peoples which they found on the spot at the time of their becoming sedentary, peoples whom they destroyed as the representative of an alien culture. . . .

As far as one can go back into Indo-European history, especially by means of comparative linguistics, only one form of patriarchal family can be found which seems to be common to all tribes before their division (Aryans, Greeks, Romans).[45]

Diop draws attention to Van Gennep's disagreement with Durkheim's interpretation of data on Australian aboriginal societies. These data, Van Gennep argued, showed many combinations of matrilineal and patrilineal descent systems. They did not show, contrary to Durkheim, a relationship of antecedence and sequence between the one and the other system. Van Gennep proposed that the tendency of European scholars to see matrilineality as antecedent and inferior to patrilineality is a consequence of the fact that European society is basically patrilineal.

Engels regarded the rise of patriarchy (patrilineal systems) as a signal of degradation in the human condition. The presumed transition from matriarchy was still, for him, a useful idea, because it confirmed that the bourgeois monogamous family, contrary to assumptions about its permanence, was a historically transient social form—as was bourgeois society as a whole. He could also explain, by historical materialist analysis, how the transition had occurred.

And yet, Diop points out, Engels did not apply materialist analysis to a critical problem in the story of ancient kinship systems: what were the material origins of matriarchy (matrilineal systems)? Were economic forces at work here? He accepted the classical explanation that under conditions of primordial sexual promiscuity and group marriage, assumed to be the earliest kin forms, maternity was always certain but paternity never could be. It follows from this that kinship could only be traced in the female line. An alternative version of this explanation is that the primitive mind does not understand the role of the father in conception. This is a proposition to which Van Gennep objected that such an assertion had never been preceded by a careful investigation into the ideas of primitives on the mechanism of conception.

Relying on this explanation, Engels did not observe that, as Diop states, "woman owes her social rank and her esteem exclusively to the structure of the society which allows her to play a leading economic role. It is unfortunate that this 'economic' factor should have escaped a Marxist."[46] Diop draws attention to the fact that in the ancient black neolithic world—Africa, the Mediterranean, Southern Europe, Western Asia, India—life was a sedentary affair based on agrarian economies. In these economies, the economic role of woman was considerable. It is this material factor that is the foundation of matrilineal systems in these societies, systems destroyed or altered after 1500 B.C. by invading white and Semitic peoples who practiced a different economic adaptation, where man was the principal provider and woman was a mouth to feed.

These early Aryans (in India), Europeans, and Semites were pastoral nomads. It is consistent that there is no record of a matrilineal past among them since there is no record either that they were ever anything but pastoral peoples in the Neolithic age.

Agrarian sedentism and pastoral nomadism are sociocultural phases that occurred after the development of plant and animal domestication. However, they are two distinct postforager adaptations with no universally determined sequential relationship between them. If, for analytic convenience, we hold all other forces constant, it can be assumed that their economic structures would generate superstructures, including kin systems, that were equally distinct.

Engels himself is well aware of the distinctness of these economic adaptations. He tells us that up to the end of the stage of savagery (hunter-gatherer society), the course of evolution had been the same for all human beings. "With the advent of barbarism, however," he continues, "we reach a stage where the difference in natural endowment of the two great continents begins to assert itself." As he conjectures, in the East (the Old World) barbarism (the Neolithic age) begins with animal domestication; in the West (the New World) it commences with plant cultivation. "The effect of these different natural conditions was that from now on the population of each hemisphere went its own special way, and the landmarks on the border lines between various stages are different in each of the two cases."[47]

For him, the different special ways are exemplified in the contrasting life-styles of the American Indians, New World peoples, and the ancient white and Semitic peoples of the Old World. The New World Neolithic Indians depended on plant cultivation. They lived in settled village communities. In the Old World, "the domestication and breeding of cattle and the formation of large herds seem to have been the cause of the differentiation of the Aryans and the Semites from the remaining mass of barbarians. Names of cattle are still common to the European and the Asiatic Aryans. The names of cultivable plants hardly at all."[48] Among these people life was pastoral.

Engels need not have gone to the New World to find peoples whose societies differed as much from the Aryan and Semitic systems as Amerindian societies did. He would have found plant cultivation and settled life in the Old World: among Dravidians and Veddoids in India and among the ancient black peoples in Nubia, Egypt, the Mediterranean, and the Near East. Consistent with the explanation that different Neolithic adaptations sent populations in the Old and New Worlds on different ways, it would be understandable that these agrarian black peoples, like the Amerindians, were evolving differently from the pastoral Aryans and Semites. And if account were taken of the disruptive incursions of these pastoralists into the southern regions of the Old World the decline of matriarchy would not have been seen simply as a transition to patriarchy.

In *The Origin of the Family,* Engels lists the assumed stages of this transition: sexual promiscuity; group marriage; the matrilineal pairing family embedded in a communistic household; the patriarchal household, incubator of male power and female submission; and the monogamian (nuclear) family, the final realization of male dominance. It was presumed that sexual promiscuity was associated with very early human groups practicing subsistence without the use of tools. By ancient times it had become culturally extinct. Group marriage belongs to the age of savagery, the pairing family to barbarism. The epoch of matriarchy embraces these three periods. It is signified in sexual equality, which Engels calls female predominance, maternity as the basis of kinship, and, with the invention of the descent group in Neolithic times, matrilineality.

The patriarchal household initiates the transition out of matriarchy. It belongs to the age of animal domestication. Its development is propelled by the growth of wealth in livestock, which replaces the hunt as the main source of food. Males appropriate this new wealth, at first within limits imposed by gentile customs, finally as private property. Ultimately, they succeed in institutionalizing patrilineal descent, a necessity if they wish to bequeath wealth to their own sons instead of their sisters' sons and other matrilineal kinfolk. The patriarchal household insists on monogamy for women, but permits concubinage for men. There is a pairing of sorts; but the pair is part of a multifamily patrilineal household under the rule of a patriarch.

With the rise of "civilization" the patriarchal household disappears and gives place to the nuclear monogamian family. The rise of the monogamian family coincides with the withdrawal of women from necessary productive work in the public sphere, which becomes the world of male activity. It is no longer easy for either partner to dissolve marriage: divorce is now the prerogative of the male. Sexual conflict matures within the unequal confines of nuclear monogamy. The first class conflict in civilized history is the antagonism that develops between man and woman in the monogamian family.

Guided by this interpretation of family evolution Engels considered the patriarchal gens of the Greeks and Romans to be at a more advanced stage of development than the matrilineal pairing family of the Amerindians—or matrilineal systems elsewhere.

"Almost two entire great periods of development," he says, "lie between the Greeks and the . . . American tribes."[49]

However, using this system of interpretation, one is unable to explain, and this is one of Diop's main criticisms, why in Africa the matrilineal descent group passed intact from barbarism to civilization. Furthermore, in African civilizations sexual equality was a fact, a fact that rested on the continuing presence of women in the public world. This is what one would expect once it is seen that African cultures, moving to their own particular rhythms, were unrelated to cultures in the Aryan and Semitic worlds. Here Diop is most original; and the data support his conclusions. Immanuel Wallerstein comments as follows:

> Diop has a theory that there is a basic global division of peoples into two kinds: the Southerners (or Negro Africans), and the Aryans (a category covering all Caucasians, including Semites, Mongoloids, and American Indians). Each grouping has a cultural outlook based on response to climate, the difference between them being that the Aryans have had a harsher climate.
>
> The Aryans have developed patriarchal systems characterized by the suppression of women and a propensity for war. Also associated with such societies are materialist religion, sin, guilt, xenophobia, the tragic drama, the city-state, individualism, and pessimism. Southerners on the other hand, are matriarchal. The women are free and the people peaceful; there is a Dionysian approach to life, religious idealism, and no concept of sin. With a matriarchal society come xenophilia, the tale as a literary form, the territorial state, social collectivism, and optimism.[50]

The contrast in systems is well drawn; and theories of universal evolution, whether derived from liberal sociology or Marxism, cannot embrace such contrasts. These theories are culture-bound. As such, they are destined to look for, or see, in other cultures what is not there—in Africa, stillborn rationalism (for liberal sociologists) or cultural stagnation (for Marxists). The thesis of a double cradle of cultural evolution clears the vision. It liberates thought from the narrow-minded presumption that everything Aryan and Semitic is culturally superior, being at a later stage in evolution, than everything African. Freed from this presumption, one sees in the late ascendancy of patriarchal systems in the ancient world the forcible displacement of matriarchal regimes by Eurasians who submerged the southern cradle during the second millennium B.C.

The Eurasian invasion of the southern cradle affected more than just the matrilineal kin systems. It affected the entire societal order of southern societies, although with differing impact. Some cultures were destroyed—Mycenaean civilization, for instance. In others, institutions retained traditional forms but functioned with stark indifference and hostility to communal well-being. The fate of Egypt under the Ptolemies represents this development. Egyptologist Margaret A. Murray offers the following description:

> The glittering facade of Alexandria as the centre of all the intellectual activity of the period has blinded the eyes of later generations to the conditions that lay behind that proud frontage.
>
> Under their native Pharaohs, the Egyptians were subject to a divine ruler to whom they and all they possessed belonged. This was, however, a personal relation; it was possible for anyone, even the poorest of the poor, to approach the god and make known his complaints. The rather happy-go-lucky method of administration suited the country, and though it depended in great measure on the personal character of the administrator in each district it was possible for the individuals of every class to attain an ordinary degree of comfort and prosperity and to live averagely happy lives. But when the Egyptian ideas were translated into the Greek concept of government, the result was disastrous. By changing the intimate relation of the Pharaoh to his people into the rule of the State which owned everybody and everything, the Greeks transformed the personal element of the Pharaonic rule into the soulless domination of State control. It was a deliberate and well-thought-out policy, carried out with efficiency and ruthlessness. Centralization and exploitation were the two principles on which the Ptolemies acted. Thus the wealth of the country came into the hands of the few, and enabled those few to build great temples inspiring wonder among visitors, and to make Alexandria the leading city for the whole of

the Near East. This was done by an adroit and crafty interpretation of the theory of the absolute authority of the Pharaoh. Theoretically the Pharaoh had been the sole owner of Egypt and all that was in it, practically he had been like most other rulers, merely the head of a country where private property and private rights were respected. But the theory was there and the Ptolemies acted on it.[51]

Such were the effects of the European assault on Africa, an assault begun in ancient times and lately completed in our epoch. These effects, and the assault itself, have not been properly appraised, or even recognized, by the intellectual traditions discussed here, with serious consequences for these traditions. Affected as well are ways of thinking, intellectual and popular, that depend on these idea systems for conception and understanding of the past, the present, and the future, and human possibilities in the broadest sense.

A few conclusions present themselves. Liberal and Marxist theories, insofar as they are comparative and historical, do not adequately take the cultural pluralism of the human universe into account. This follows from the mistaken interpretations they offer of Africa and the black worlds. The argument I offer in this chapter has dealt with errors in scientific interpretation. The brief discussion of structure and dynamics of African society suggests what the traditions criticized here have missed.

Certain features of African society require emphasis: the vitality of the moral underpinning of social behavior, the unshakable institutional commitment to communal welfare enshrined by moral tradition, and the limits traditionally set on the use of power as a tool of ruling-class or personal interests. It is these features that made it possible, as Margaret Murray says in the passage just cited, for Africans "of every class to attain an ordinary degree of comfort and prosperity and to live averagely happy lives."

There are many who feel uncertain about hope for a future free from the threatening disorders of modern industrial civilization. Imprisoned in the historical misinterpretations I have described, they have not seen anything in past civilizations that can give substance to dreams. To such as these, it is instructive to note that African culture created and maintained civilizations that were humanistic. This fact is concealed not simply by intellectual and cognitive error, but also by ethnocentric and racist white thinking. If the mind can be freed of these fetters, African societies might appear not just as firm ground for historical optimism, but also as models that moderns would wish to emulate.

Rethinking history along lines implied by the argument I have presented—especially identifying black anteriority anthropologically and culturally—elevates blackness. This must have an immeasurably positive impact on black peoples today. But it is not only good for blacks. Such revision is a contribution to a view of history as it actually happened. This can only be good for everybody.

CONCLUSION

MY STATED intent in the preceding discussion was to draw forth the real Africa—its culture, its past, its contributions to human experience—from behind the Eurocentric haze that veils it. I hope I have met this purpose. I also suggested that the African data could give answers to certain puzzles that beset contemporary life—most important, the origins of the frightful levels of modern violence.

One school of thought tells us that social ills, antihuman violence in particular, are rooted in innate human depravity. The counterargument is that these ills have cultural origins. The weight of voluminous data on primitive life contradicts the thesis of innate human evil. Ethnographic accounts almost invariably paint a picture of primitive life as peaceful. The conclusion is inescapable that humankind has had a long history of peace, because, for most of that history, life was lived in primitive settings.

The source of primitive peacefulness is not mysterious. Anthropologists identify the absence of property relations in land, plant and animal life, and the basic resources of nature; the institutional practice of sharing and reciprocity; the governance of ethics and etiquette; and the all-pervasive embrace of kinship relations as the foundations of peaceful life in primitive society. The structural effect of sharing, reciprocity, and the absence of property is that the social classes in primitive society (men and women, married and unmarried, young and old) are not stratified; these classes are simply nonhierarchical, functional groupings within the division of labor. Cultural analysis reveals that there is no ground for conflict and violence. That is why these ills do not afflict primitive life.

The critical exercise I have conducted in these chapters accepts the idea that human behavior is culturally determined. It also accepts primitive social equality as, by now, axiomatic historical fact. However, this is evidently not an axiom in theories that propose the universality of stratification. Moreover these theories, and functionalism for one, accept cultural determinism.

The Marxist tradition rescued primitive life from liberal misinterpretation. It did not do the same for African civilizations. I have discussed the mistakes of the Marxist interpretation: it misread the stability of African systems as stagnation; it did not grasp that these systems have their own distinctive historical motion; it did not recognize European disruption of Africa in ancient times; and it made European imperialism historically, that is to say, morally, justifiable.

Misreading of primitive life is of a piece with misreading of African, and Third World, histories and cultures. On the basis of such misreadings, it is possible to criticize the poverty of historical imagination in Western social thought. Western thought is an inadequate tool when one is dealing with questions of human fate, for instance, determining a historically accurate phenomenology of violence, social evil, and social inequality.

Social inequality is not universal. Primitive society proves that. Still, as the liberal argument can be read, is it not inevitable in complex systems, along with the social tensions it produces? Or will it disappear when, according to Marx, the state transforms into an administrative machine? Then, is bureaucratic power in socialist societies today to be understood as a transient phenomenon on the road to administratively managed equality? And if one is not convinced about this last proposition, must one not accept the proposition that inequality and social evil will forever be part of the human condition?

Given the structure of state society this is a pointless argument: it poses a choice between nonexistent alternatives. Civilizations are social systems with a complex division of labor, structured social differentiation, and a state machinery as paramount agency of control. The state is never purely administrative. It is always an agency of power: it claims a monopoly of violence and a monopoly of power over life and death. It makes no sense to imagine the disappearance of the state in complex social formations. The question is whether social peace is possible in such systems.

The history of African civilizations testifies that such peace is possible. I have discussed their longevity. The fact that ordinary, as opposed to elite, Africans could achieve modest prosperity and comfort and lead averagely happy lives has been emphasized as the critical factor behind the stability of these systems. Security of individual lives was not a fortuitous outcome. As I have described, African states were stratified, but they were not driven by insoluble structural antagonisms, and communal and individual well-being was the precise aim of statecraft. Those who held power were kept to this aim by constitutional restraints; and, most important, were committed to such well-being as a traditional moral imperative. All of this permits the conclusion that there is no inevitable relationship between stratification, conflict, and social disorder. Whether or not there is social peace or social conflict depends on the cultural management of stratification and the cultural definition of the aim and proper use of power.

I have stressed the point, following Diop, that Africa is the cradle of the evolution and world dispersion of a cultural style different from the European one. The hegemonic rise of Europe has been hostile to Africa, Africans, and African traditions. Despite that, African traditions have survived into our time even through the unholy travails of modern slavery, modern imperialism and neo-imperialism, and racial oppression. Although they have been deeply affected by European cultural styles, they have inspired lifeways that suggest what a humanistic resurrection of modern life could be.

Blacks have rhythm, they say in America. Verily. But one must add, they brought it with them. Old World, African rhythms are at the basis of all rhythmic music emanating from the New World today. The tango, samba, mambo, salsa, calypso, reggae, rhythm and blues, rap, jazz, and fusion have transformed the musical sensibilities of the planet. Rhythm is not simply a property of music. It moves, and it removes—that is why one feels good. It moves the body, it moves the mind, not simply to dance but to feel. There is rhythmic feel in walk, in talk, in work, in play, in all aspects of black American life. Rhythm is central in black religion. Black religion expresses itself in celebrant worship.

If religion is an institutional repository of ultimate values, then it must be said that for black people, even under the conditions of their existence in America, the celebration of life is an ultimate value. In place of the antagonistic and acquisitive frenzy that drives Western culture it offers different aims for life's energies. Were such aims to inform the cultural mind, would that alter the conduct of politics in a humanistic direction? The political history of black Americans, the very people who brought celebrant traditions to America, suggests this possibility.

It is suggested in a commitment to nonviolent struggle that has persisted through three hundred years of black resistance. It is a principled commitment and should not be understood simply as sensible political pragmatism, as something that is well advised for a clearly outnumbered minority. Certainly slave rebels and urban rioters did not consider it pragmatic. The movie, *Ragtime,* presents a scene of deep drama in which Booker T. Washington (played by Moses Gunn) asserts nonviolence as principle. He observes that violent resistance perpetuates unending violence. It is the destiny of black people, he asserts, to end strife and bring peace to America.

Booker T. Washington is not, was not in his time, beyond criticism. But he was correct in this: the black vision of power is peace. That vision appears briefly during Reconstruction, the only period of black ascendancy in American history—and significant if only for this reason. Southern constitutions of the time were the product of damaging compromises that black delegates, in order to hold power, had to concede to white allies who regarded them at best as necessary evils. Even so these constitutions reversed the time-honored practice of excluding the majority, black and white, from representation in and control of government. Poor whites and women were given privileges long denied them. Protection against imprisonment for debt, protection of small land holdings from expropriation (a boon to poor whites who in the main were the small landholders of the period), the first right of women to divorce, the security against seizure of the property of women for their husbands' indebtedness, public education at public expense, government responsibility for and participation in the founding and maintenance of agencies of social welfare—these constitute the record.[1] Compromised by necessity though it was, black power appears as a government of and for the downtrodden, which indeed makes it consistent with very ancient traditions.

There is a coda. White Southerners, especially the old planter aristocrats, had no stomach for the spectacle of black power come to the Southern legislatures. Many had nightmarish fears of black retribution. But no vengeance was ever visited on them.

South Carolina, with a majority of black voters and state legislators, and with blacks holding posts in state, county, and town bureaucracies, was considered a black paradise. But it was not a white hell. White women, an observer noted, went about with a sense of ease, as though black men were not in power. Until the white counterrevolution blacks and whites enjoyed friendly, peaceable relations in the many contexts of social life. As it never had before, the state prospered.

Reconstruction was a time of black exhilaration. Clearly, that mood did not depend on vengeful treatment of those who had oppressed black people. It was generated by the widening horizons political power seemed to promise for the race; the chance the time offered that all citizens, especially those of humble origins, would thrive; and, one must add, the vision of a peaceable life for the national community.

African traditions, we may strongly urge from all this, are not fossilized artifacts in the historical consciousness. They are treated as such by those who look at them through Western, or Westernized, eyes. For those who can see clearly, these traditions are the necessary foundation of black identity within the American ethnic mix and a resource for the creative restructuring of the social order; but they are, as it were, a silent and unacknowledged foundation. It would be fruitful for blacks and all people interested in historical truth to explore further the vital affinities connecting African traditions with contemporary black political and social life. One would discover that they present to the imagination something other than Anglo-Saxon techno-logic— if only one has the courage to see it.

NOTES

Introduction

1. Eleanor Burke Leacock, *Myths of Male Dominance* (New York: Monthly Review Press, 1981), Preface and Introduction.

2. Ibid., p. 14.

3. For a fuller account of this intellectual and social odyssey, see the appendix to my doctoral dissertation, "Behind the Eurocentric Veils," Sociology, Brandeis University, 1988.

1. Mainstream Thinking and Modern Life

1. Ruth Benedict, *Patterns of Culture* (Boston: Houghton Mifflin, 1934), 11.

2. The following books give an overview of the conduct of Europeans in the colonies: Chinua Achebe, *Things Fall Apart* (New York: Fawcett, 1969); Joseph Conrad, *Heart of Darkness* (New York: New American Library, n.d.); D. K. Fieldhouse, *The Colonial Empires* (New York: Delacorte Press, 1967); and E. D. Morel, *The Black Man's Burden* (New York and London: Monthly Review Press, 1969).

3. William Ryan, *Blaming the Victim* (New York: Random House, 1971), 26.

4. See ch. 1, "The Art of Savage Discovery," in ibid., esp. 25–29.

5. André Gunder Frank, "The Development of Underdevelopment," in Robert I. Rhodes, ed., *Imperialism and Underdevelopment* (New York and London: Monthly Review Press, 1970), 4.

6. Benedict, 6–7, 271.

7. George W. Stocking, Jr., *Race, Culture, and Evolution* (New York: The Free Press, 1968); see 172–94 for discussion of Boas on hybrid fertility and intergenerational change among immigrants, and 157–60 for Boas on sound blindness.

8. Ibid., 213.

9. Racism, however, it hardly need be said, did not disappear, so deeply rooted beneath the bright surface of rational awareness. On the subject of racism in Western culture, with the focus on America, consult Joel Kovel, *White Racism: A Psychohistory* (New York: Random House, 1971). See esp. ch. 8, "The Psychohistory of Racism in the United States."

10. G. W. F. Hegel, *The Philosophy of History* (New York: Dover Publication, 1956), 99.

11. Max Weber, *The Theory of Social and Economic Organization,* trans. A. M. Henderson and Talcott Parsons (New York: The Free Press, 1964), 337–38, 339.

12. Talcott Parsons, *The Social System* (New York: The Free Press, 1961), 499.

13. Gabriel Almond and James Coleman, eds., *The Politics of the Developing Areas* (Princeton: Princeton University Press, 1960), 17.

14. Ibid., 23.

15. Gabriel Almond and Sidney Verba, *The Civic Culture* (Boston and Toronto: Little, Brown and Co., 1965), 4.

16. Jerome Skolnick and Elliot Currie, eds., *Crisis in American Institutions* (Boston and Toronto: Little, Brown and Co., 1979).

17. Richard L. Rubenstein, *The Cunning of History: The Holocaust and the American Future* (New York: Harper and Row, 1975), 7.

18. Ibid., 8.

19. Lorna Marshall, "Kung Bushmen Bands," in R. Cohen and J. Middleton, eds., *Comparative Political Systems* (New York: Natural History Press, 1967), 18.

20. Colin Clark, "Population Growth and Living Standards," in A. N. Agarwala and S. P. Singh, eds., *The Economics of Underdevelopment* (New York: Oxford University Press, 1973), 46.

21. See William J. Goode, *World Revolution and Family Patterns* (London: The Free Press, 1963), 50–52. There is an ironic turnaround to Malthusian principles in the data on industrial populations. While it is true that fertility rates are lower the higher one ascends the stratification system, in each class those who are well off bear more children than those who are not.

22. Rubenstein, 104.

23. Ibid., 9. Emphasis in original.

24. Philip Slater, *The Pursuit of Loneliness* (Boston: Beacon Press, 1970), xii.

25. Mirra Komarovsky, *Blue-Collar Marriage* (New York: Random House, 1962), 346.

26. Ibid., 284.

27. See Rubenstein, ch. 2.

28. Ibid., chs. 4 and 6.

29. Slater, 40–41.

30. Rubenstein, 31.

31. By sentimentality, I mean the liberal wish for social reform conjoined with dogmatic faith in basic institutional processes. It is an attitude of victim blamers, those who, as William Ryan said, like the society pretty much the way it is, although as Christian or liberal humanitarians, they regret its socially ugly aspects as unfortunate—but unavoidable.

32. Quoted in Kovel, 139.

2: And What about the Radical Alternative?

1. Herbert Marcuse, *Reason and Revolution* (Boston: Beacon Press, 1960), 276.

2. Max Weber, *The Theory of Social and Economic Organization*, trans. A. M. Henderson and Talcott Parsons (New York: The Free Press, 1964), 185.

3. Ibid. Leslie White has a similar point of view: "We mean by ethics a code of rules the purpose of which is to regulate the behavior of individuals so that the Welfare, or what is deemed to be welfare, of the group will be fostered. We define welfare in terms of subsistence, health, protection from the elements, defense against enemies, etc.; in short, in terms of security and continuity of life." Leslie White, *The Evolution of Culture* (New York: McGraw-Hill, 1959), 216–17.

4. Shlomo Avineri, ed., *Karl Marx on Colonialism and Modernization* (New York: Anchor Books, 1969), 13.

5. Karl Marx, Preface to *A Contribution to the Critique of Political Economy*, in Marx and Engels, *Selected Works* (1968; reprint, New York: International Publishers, 1980), 183.

6. Karl Marx, *Pre-capitalist Economic Formations*, ed. E. J. Hobsbawm (New York: International Publishers, 1965), 67.

7. Marx, "The British Rule in India," in Avineri, 94.

8. Marx, *Pre-capitalist Economic Formations*, 94, 96.

9. Ibid., 91.

10. Ibid.

11. Ibid., 94.

12. Ibid., 68.

13. Ibid., 84–85 (emphasis in original).

14. From "Ignazio Silone," in Richard Crossman, ed., *The God That Failed* (New York: Harper and Brothers, 1949), 79–80.

15. Ralph Ellison, *Invisible Man* (New York: New American Library, 1952), 408–9.

16. Crossman, "Introduction," in *The God That Failed*, 3.

17. George Padmore, *Pan-Africanism or Communism* (New York: Doubleday, 1972), 270.

18. "Communist power politics apart, the Russian people are undoubtedly the least colour-conscious white folk in the world. The coloured Soviet citizens of Central Asia—Uzbekians, Tajiks, Kazans, Turkmans, Tartars, Kirghizans, Chuvashians, Kalmuks, Buriats, etc.—enjoy absolute racial equality with those of Slav descent. If they are sometimes persecuted, it is not for their race as are the non-Europeans—Africans, Indians, Coloureds—in South Africa, but for political 'deviations.' . . . The Soviet leaders, whatever may be said against them, treat any manifestation of racial chauvinism with great severity." Ibid., 292. The explosion of anti-Soviet unrest among non-Russian nationalities might make Padmore seem a political romantic. Padmore's own qualifiers, however, should be kept in mind—"on the whole," "the least colour-conscious white folk." It should also be kept in mind that blacks, whether native (Abkhazians, other blacks from the Black Sea region) or foreign (Americans, Africans, or West Indians) would in general give a parallel assessment, more than likely with the same qualifiers. "What has most impressed Negroes about Russian society is the absence of institutionalized racism. There may be racist individuals; but if detected these persons are subject to crushing public opprobrium." Allison Blakely, *Russia and the Negro: Blacks in Russian History and Thought* (Washington, D.C.: Howard University Press, 1986), 166. If Padmore were alive and could speak, it is certain he would support the anti-Soviet demands of non-Russian nationalities today. His book, after all, is the manifesto of a revolutionary nationalist.

19. For Halonen's argument, see Harold Cruse, *The Crisis of the Negro Intellectual* (New York: William Morrow, 1967), 137.

20. Ibid.

21. On Calverton, see ibid., 158–60.

22. Ibid., 146.

23. Ibid., 158.

24. Padmore, 320.

3. For Those Who Think Black Studies Can Be Too Nationalistic

1. Apropos of this point George Stocking writes: "The 'lower' races were still the 'uncivilized' or 'savage' ones, the races with darker skins. Civiliza-

tion, on the other hand was still synonymous with European society, which was the society of white men, of Caucasians. In the literature of the social sciences, the identification of Caucasian and civilized man was implied or assumed more often than it was stated, but the implication was frequently all too clear. . . . In turn-of-the-century evolutionary thinking, savagery, dark skin, and a small brain and incoherent mind, were for many all part of the single evolutionary picture of 'primitive' man, who even yet walked the earth." George W. Stocking, Jr., *Race, Culture, and Evolution* (New York: The Free Press, 1968), 131–32. How this idea took root in European thought is described on pp. 34–41.

2. Ibid., 46.

3. What follows is taken from Marcellin Boule and Henri V. Vallois, *Fossil Men* (London: Thames and Hudson, 1957), ch. 8, esp. 278–92.

4. Ibid., 285, 289, 287–88.

5. Ibid., 289.

6. Quoted in Cheikh Anta Diop, *The African Origin of Civilization* (1955; reprint, New York: Lawrence Hill, 1974), 262.

7. Ibid., 263.

8. Boule and Vallois, 449, 319.

9. Diop, 268.

10. John Geipel, *The Europeans* (London: Longmans and Green, 1969), 19. This author thinks the "hooded" female figure from Brassempouy is Asiatic because of the slanted eyes of the figure. The hair, though braided, seems straight to him. That may be, but Chancelade Man, prototype of Asiatic peoples, appears in the Magdalenian period, whereas the statue is Aurignacian. See also Joseph Birdsell, *Human Evolution* (Chicago: Rand McNally, 1975), 330–31, for the fertility symbol interpretation and the argument reinterpreting the prognathism of the Grimaldi skulls.

11. Boule and Vallois, 292.

12. Quoted from LeGrand H. Clegg II, "Ancient America: A Missing Link in Black History," *A Current Bibliography on African Affairs* (May 1972), in James Spady, "Afterword," in Cheikh Anta Diop, *The Cultural Unity of Black Africa* (1959; reprint, Chicago: Third World Press, 1978), 209.

13. For what follows see Olivia Vlahos, *African Beginnings* (New York: Viking Press, 1967), 25–29, 43–46.

14. This is only part of the list enumerated and discussed in Diop, *African Origin*, ch. 7. This book and Diop's *The Cultural Unity of Black Africa* are essential reading for anyone looking for a comprehensive exposition and rebuttal of a long litany of anti-African Egyptological writings.

15. James H. Breasted, *A History of Egypt* (New York: Charles Scribner's Sons, 1912), 26.

16. E. Wallis Budge, *A History of the Egyptian People* (London: J. M. Dent and Sons, 1914), 13.

17. Diop, *African Origin,* 51.

18. The discussion that follows is taken from Edith R. Sanders, "Rape of African History: The Hamitic Hypothesis," *Liberator* 10, no. 4 (April 1970).

19. Ibid., 9.

20. Diop, *African Origin,* chs. 3–5.

21. See John G. Jackson, *Introduction to African Civilization* (New York: University Books, 1970), 66; and William Leo Hansberry, "Ancient Kush, Old Aethiopia, and the Balad Es Sudan," *Journal of Human Relations* 8 (1960): 367.

22. What follows is adapted from Harry L. Shapiro, "The Jewish People: A Biological History," in *Race and Science,* UNESCO papers on "The Race Question in Modern Science" (New York: Columbia University Press, 1961).

23. Ibid., 115.

24. See Jackson, ch. 2; and Diop, *Cultural Unity,* 106–11. The quotation is from *Cultural Unity,* 106–7.

25. Jackson, 73–74.

26. Ibid., 75.

27. Translator's preface in Diop, *African Origin,* and 230–31.

28. For this point, see George G. M. James, *Stolen Legacy* (reprint, San Francisco: Julian Richardson Associates, 1976).

29. Basil Davidson, *The African Genius* (Boston: Little, Brown and Co., 1969), 67.

30. Diop, *African Origin,* 156.

31. L. S. B. Leakey, *The Progress and Evolution of Man in Africa* (London: Oxford University Press, 1961), 20.

32. See Diop, *African Origin,* 162.

33. Basil Davidson, *Africa in History* (1968; reprint, New York: Macmillan, 1974), 28.

34. Ibid., 231.

35. See Chancellor Williams, *The Destruction of Black Civilization* (Chicago: Third World Press, 1976), 174.

36. Davidson, *The African Genius,* 75–76.

37. Vlahos, 133.

38. Williams, 174–75.

39. The ideas that follow are condensed from Paul Kirchhoff, "The Principles of Clanship in Human Society," in Morton H. Fried, ed., *Readings in Anthropology,* vol. 2, 2d ed. (New York: Thomas Y. Crowell, 1968).

40. Davidson, *The African Genius,* 82, 83; similar observations are made in Williams, 172–80.

41. Davidson, *The African Genius,* 70.

42. "Introduction," in M. Fortes and E. E. Evans-Pritchard, eds., *African Political Systems* (London: Oxford University Press, 1940), 8.

43. "It should be remembered that in these states there is only one theory of government. In the event of rebellion, the aim, and result, is only to change the personnel of office and never to abolish it or to substitute for it some new form of government. When subordinate chiefs, who are often kinsmen of the king, rebel against him they do so in defense of the values violated by his malpractices." Ibid., 13.

44. Davidson, *The African Genius,* 191.

45. Diop, *Cultural Unity,* 27–28.

46. Ibid., 35.

47. Frederick Engels, *The Origin of the Family, Private Property, and the State,* in Karl Marx and Frederick Engels, *Selected Works* (New York: International Publishers, 1980), 470–71.

48. Ibid., 471.

49. Ibid., 530.

50. Diop, Introduction, *African Origin,* x.

51. Margaret A. Murray, *The Splendour That Was Egypt,* rev. ed. (New York: Praeger, 1964), 59–60.

Conclusion

1. See Lerone Bennett, Jr., *Black Power U.S.A.: The Human Side of Reconstruction,* 1867–1877 (Chicago: Johnson, 1967).